EX LIBRIS

Kristen L. Johnson

The Teddy Bear Book

by
Peter Bull

Random House New York

Published in the United States
by Random House, Inc., New York.
Distributed in Canada
by Random House of Canada Limited, Toronto.
Originally published in Great Britain by
Hutchinson & Co. Ltd., London.
Library of Congress Catalog Card Number: 77-85556
ISBN 0-394-73080-1
Manufactured in the United States of America
9 8 7 6 5 4 3 2

Acknowledgments

Acknowledgment is gratefully extended to the following for permission to reprint from their works:

BRIDESHEAD REVISITED, by Evelyn Waugh, Copyright 1944, 1945, by Evelyn Waugh. Reprinted by permission of Little, Brown and Company.

LOOK BACK IN ANGER, by John Osborne, Copyright © 1957 by S. G. Phillips, Inc., and Faber and Faber.

COMPULSION, by Meyer Levin, Copyright © 1959 by Meyer Levin. Reprinted by permission of Simon & Schuster.

TOYS IN AMERICA, by Marshall and Inex McLintock. Reprinted by permission of the Public Affairs Press.

THE BOOK OF THE TEDDY BEAR, by Margaret Hutchings. Reprinted by permission of Mills & Boon, Ltd.

Article by Robert Pitman. Reprinted by permission of the SUNDAY EXPRESS, London.

SUMMONED BY BELLS, by John Betjeman. Reprinted by permission of Houghton Mifflin Company and John Murray Ltd.

From the book WINNIE-THE-POOH, by A. A. Milne. Drawings by E. H. Shepard. Copyright 1926 by E. P. Dutton, Inc. Renewal, 1954, by A. A. Milne. Reprinted by permission of the publishers.

THE CURIOUS SAVAGE, by John Patrick. Copyright 1950, 1951 by John Patrick. Reprinted by permission of the author and the Dramatists Play Service, Inc.

Extract from the December 1967 WHICH? The Magazine of the Consumers' Association. Reprinted by permission of the publishers, Consumers' Association, 14 Buckingham Street, London, WC 2.

AN OCTOPUS IN MY HEAD, by Jean Deverson. Reprinted by permission of the publisher Leslie Frewin.

Excerpt from "I Wish I Had a Teddy Bear." Reprinted by permission of Galliard Ltd. "The Sick Teddy Bear" from MORE KIDDIES by Daisy McGeogh. Reprinted by permission of Leonard, Gould & Bolttler, London.

Lyrics from "Me and My Teddy Bear" by Jack Winters and J. Fred Coots, Copyright © 1950 by Chappell & Co., Inc. Used by permission.

Thanks are also due to the following for use of their material: Keystone Press; THE SUN; THE WASHINGTON POST; DAILY RECORD; THE HANOVER GAZETTE; REDBRIDGE RECORDER; YARMOUTH MERCURY; EASTERN DAILY PRESS; The Bettman Archives; Theodore Roosevelt Association, Courtesy American Heritage; Photoworld; Brown Brothers; THE SURREY ADVERTISER; 20th-Century Fox; Columbia Pictures; London Weekend Television; Action for the Crippled Child; Foote, Cone & Belding; Georg Jensen Inc.; Abraham & Straus.

I wish to thank the following for their invaluable contributions: Mrs. Joy Anderson; Miss Jonquil Anthony; Miss Audley; Lady Barran; the late Mr. Clifford Berryman; Sir John Betjeman, C. B. E.; Mr. George Burke; Mrs. Iris Butler; Mrs. Carr; Mrs. Harvey Childs; Miss Dinah Cody; "Ted" Cooper; Mr. and Mrs. Daly; Miss Ann Daubercies; Sir Gangy de Brownman, Baronet; *The Roosevelt Bears* by Seymour Eaton; Mrs. Howard Fenton; Miss Marilyn Franconero; Mr. David Frankel; Mrs. Freestone; Mrs. Fowler; H. M. Gayforth; Miss Jacqueline Geldart; Mrs. Richard Hadley; Mrs. Heelas; Lieut.-Colonel Henderson; Mrs. James; Mrs. Johnson; Mr. Kaigh Kabell; Mr. John Kobal; Mrs. Leggett; Mr. Karl Lehner, the Curator of the Alpine Museum, Zermatt; "Ted" Lewin; Mrs. Cynthia Lindsay; Miss Deirdre Mackinnon; Miss Helen MacLachlan, the Curator of the Theodore Roosevelt Birthplace; Mrs. Pauline Marrian; Mrs. James Dow McCallum; Mrs. Helen Lovejoy McCarthy; Miss Betty McDermid and Shad; the late Mr. Russell McLean (The "Teddy Bear Man"); Lieutenant H. M. Mears; Miss Maren Mendenhall; Mr. Benjamin Michtom of the Ideal Toy Corporation of America; "Ted Moore"; Mr. Matthew Murphy; Archibald Ormsby-Gore, Esq.; Mrs. Joan Paton; Mr. John Pitt, DSC.; Miss Elizabeth Rimer; Mrs. Judith Robins; Mrs. Gillian Robinson; Miss Jean Scott Rogers; Mrs. Edith Roseveare; Mrs. Hugh St. Paul; Miss Winifred Seaton and "Buzzy"; Mrs. Marty Simmons; Mrs. Eulia Smith-Zimman; Miss Easter Straker; Mrs. Winifred Sugg; the late Mr. Peter Swanwick; Mrs. Thayer; Miss Thonger; Miss Jennie Wade; Mrs. Orlando Wagner; Mrs. Helen Walton and One-Eyed Connolly; Mr. I. Warshaw; Mrs. Bridget Wastre; Major A. M. Watson, The Royal Military Academy Sandhurst (Paratroop Regiment); Miss Rosemary Weir; Mr. Gregory Wilson, the Curator of the Theodore Roosevelt Collection, Harvard College Library; Miss Winder; Mrs. Wrist; Miss Katherine Young; Mr. Lawrence Zimmerman; Mr. Desmond Zwar.

And to add my sincere gratitude to Ronald Monroe, Don Lawrence, Patrick Woodcock, Steven M. L. Aronson, and above all, Rachael Feild for their constant help, encouragement, and sage counsel.

For T. Edward and Theodore particularly
with love and gratitude,
and for all their friends and relations

Contents

Bears

I love my little Teddy Bear,
He's such a friendly fellow,
His fur, beautiful and soft,
Is neither brown nor yellow.
He plays but never quarrels with me,
And keeps me gay and jolly,
And I don't have to punish him
As often as my Dolly.
He's such a quiet little chap,
No impish schemes he hatches,
He never barks, he has no fleas,
At least he never scratches.

Eulia Smith-Zimman

The
Teddy Bear
Book

Foreword

It all started, I suppose, one evening a few years ago in New York, when a group of us were discussing childhood traumas. Suddenly a beautiful lady I've known for a very long time launched into a quite horrifying reminiscence.

At the age of eight she was traveling across Europe with her parents on one of those luxury express trains. At some frontier or other, Customs officials came aboard and rigorously examined everybody's luggage. One of the men caught sight of a Teddy Bear, which my friend had carried all the way from London. He snatched it from her, slit it smartly down the stomach, and tore its head from its body. The child, not unnaturally, screamed the train down and would not be comforted. It was useless for her parents to explain that the men were searching for contraband: the harm was done, the incident indelible, and she has never had the heart to acquire another Teddy Bear. As she spoke, the sickening tale was re-created so vividly that her listeners, like herself, have been unable to erase it from memory. I know that I have often thought of it with a shudder.

Yet at the time my main feeling was astonishment that I was not the only person in the world with a Teddy Bear secret, mine being that my mother had disposed of my beloved friend one term-time to a local rummage sale. She had done this without my permission or knowledge, and this made me sit and sulk throughout the holidays, fiercely resenting the fact that this cherished symbol of security had been so thoughtlessly discarded. I was sixteen at the time and felt sure that any display of emotion would be regarded as unmanly. But I have since discovered that age has nothing to do with that. Only recently a friend of mine, aged circa thirty-five, had an appalling row with his mother, not because of the peculiar behavior of his eccentric wife in her house, but because he'd been unable to locate his Teddy Bear there. His mother eventually confessed that she'd given it to the garbage men.

Until a few years ago the whole subject of one's toys (adult and childhood) was such a private and personal affair that I never thought of probing more generally into the subject. But encouraged by additional startling disclosures, I began to prompt people for similar memories of their youth, and it very soon dawned on me that there were (a) enough people with fascinating material to divulge about Teddy Bears and (b) a sufficiently large potential public to welcome a book about them.

On my return to London, I decided to try my luck. I put an ad in the Personal Columns of *The Times* (fortunately still on the front page in those days) which read: "History of E. Bear Esquire. Reminiscences, Data, Photographs (returnable) urgently required by Peter Bull, who is compiling a symposium on these remarkable creatures. No actual bears, thank you!"

Clearly my hunch was right. Letters began to pour in, to such an extent that I had to engage a secretary to deal with them. And when I made a couple of TV appearances and spoke on the radio as a result of public interest, several newspapers took up the cause and the material grew in strength and variety.

But I still couldn't visualize the construction, format, or shape of the book I had in mind. I was fully aware that Margaret Hutchings had written *The Book of The Teddy Bear* (published by Mills and Boon in England in 1964), and a delightful book it was. And don't think I'm not going to borrow shamelessly from it. But the bulk of her book is devoted to the art of actually making a Teddy Bear and supplying him with wardrobe and props. Now is the moment to warn you that you must be fully prepared for Teddy's sex to change from page to page. I will refer to him mostly as "he," though every now and then an obviously female bear will crop up. A lot of people, however, regard him as an "it." That's one of the things I've spent my life trying to avoid.

I wanted to do the book in the form of a general tribute, but I wanted to make it a very personal book, too — by describing the effect and influence that the Teddy Bear has exerted over the man, woman, and child in the street. Or the home, come to think of it. I didn't want to do it analytically, by searching for hidden meanings and digging about in people's subconsciouses. The bears would hate that. Imagine their faces if I were to tell them they were being labeled Case History Number a hundred and something!

No, I just wanted to set down in print treasured memories of the stuffed animal, whether they were happy or sad.

As in my case, I knew that many people would have kept quiet about various aspects of their childhood, for fear of ridicule or frank disbelief. I deplore this because it is desperately important to have something to cling to—to remind you of the days when life seemed to be uncomplicated—days constructed entirely for your enjoyment and entertainment, when meals were set in front of you as if by magic and you never had to be in a Certain Place at a Certain Time. Or if you did, Certain People took you there. Above all, you were aware that there was always somebody to tell your joys and sorrows to, and in far more cases than I had ever realized, this someone was Teddy Bear.

You'll see that the emotion felt by some adults when discussing their stuffed animals is pretty intense. Many, like me, feel a kind of human fellowship with them. If we ever organize a gigantic rally of Teddies and their owners (of which more later), I bet that the average age of those attending, both humans and animals, will be nearer fifty than five.

As I spread my net for material wider, I heard about bears on safari, mountain-climbing bears, far-flung Empire bears, theatre mascot bears, bears who had defected from Iron Curtain countries and had been found demanding political asylum in obscure Swiss hotels, law-breaking bears and peace-making bears, bears with squeaking ears and growling hips, homemade bears and even one who had been let down on a string to shake the hand of Theodore Roosevelt in person! A historic moment this must have been, for it was this President of the United States who was responsible for the whole dotty, marvelous mystique of the Teddy Bear. A lot of you may know that, but in the next chapter you will learn exactly how he was responsible for all the tralala.

Until not very long ago I was fully convinced that the Teddy Bear was one of our English inventions. To go with English Muffins, English Nannies, Toad in the Hole, Shepherd's Pie, and Nursery Teas. Well, it was a bit of a shock, I'm telling you, to find that there was hardly a shred of evidence to support this theory. But the actual facts of Teddy's American origin got more and more conflicting, and it soon became clear that I would have to pursue the conundrum to this side of the Atlantic.

It was Providence at this particular moment that offered me the role of a pukka British colonel in the New York production of Peter Shaffer's highly risible *Black Comedy*. And when I was not inside the late Miss Ethel Barrymore's Theatre, falling out of a rocking chair twice nightly (four times on matinee days), I found that I had plenty of time to launch a frontal attack on American Arctophilists.*

Oddly enough, I found myself getting nowhere. Didn't Americans care about Teddy Bears, too? However, I *was* cheered to discover that a close friend had hidden his under the floorboards of his parents' house to ensure his safety.

"But isn't he lonely?" I asked.

"Not a bit," replied my chum cheerfully. "He's got a lot of old love letters to look at and plenty of hard-core pornography."

What was I to do? I didn't have the nerve to go up to people in the street and ask them if they had had a Teddy Bear and were still hanging on to him like grim death. After all, possession of a Teddy Bear after a certain age is a very private matter indeed.

I had made a series of abortive radio broadcasts, and was beginning really to despair, when quite suddenly Opportunity Knocked in the guise of the *Today* TV program. I was given a marvelous "spot" at the end (8:30 A.M., the ideal time to catch everybody on the hop), and Hugh Downs, who interviewed me, did it all so well that I was allowed to talk my head off without too much self-consciousness.

I had been allowed to bring my family of bears (all fourteen of

*Friends of the bear.

Teddy Bears' picnic in Berkeley Square, London

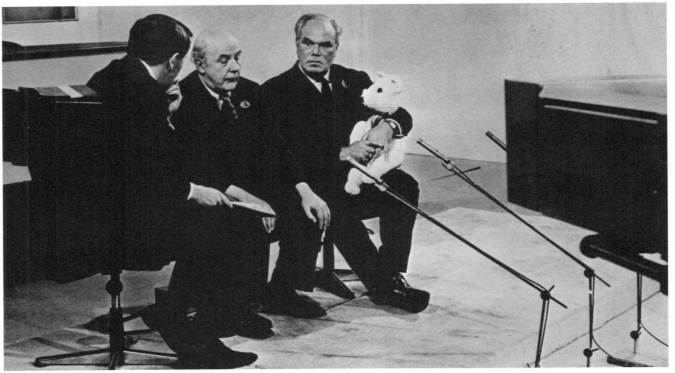

David Frost interviews Sir John Betjeman, Peter Bull and Snowy

them). The studio people wanted them to be left overnight on the stage so that they could be set to their best advantage. I had to agree, though Theodore, my eldest and most precious Teddy friend, refused point blank to go and I had to take him in my pocket the next morning. The others were in a foul temper when I greeted them, since they, too, hate being away from base without me.

But the effect of their appearance on the small screen was sensational! Hundreds of letters poured in, and soon I was realizing how *totally* different this fresh material was from its British counterpart.

The sort of letter to which I had grown accustomed in my native land gaily related incidents of bears being fumigated in ovens or soaked in disinfectant to destroy germs, only to be loved more dearly afterwards. There were tales of horrid brothers setting beloved animals adrift on duck ponds, but most of these had happy endings.

The greater part of the American mail provided examples of far more serious involvement. Many letter-writers used me as their analytical couch, but in a country where psychiatric treatment is tax-deductible, you have to be prepared for anything.

Glued to my desk in Morningside Heights — when, that is, I was not acting in the evenings and on two afternoons a week — I was flabbergasted by the violence of much of the material. I could not reconcile myself to the fact that the seemingly innocuous Teddy could have been personally responsible for so many family feuds, broken marriages and engagements, alcoholic binges, and even suicides.

But fortunately, after Theodore's next appearance (this time on the *Tonight* show with Mr. Johnny Carson), he accumulated a mass of cheerful personal fan mail, which I, as his full-time secretary, had to answer.

Among the many presents sent to him, the most touching was a small companion. He was one and a half inches high and at least a head shorter than Theodore himself. The visitor arrived in a very ancient tin box which had SOAP written on it. His owner had seen Theodore on the television screen and got the idea that her old friend, who had spent most of his life in a sewing basket, would be happy with him.

They do, in fact, get on famously and have invested in a private airplane to facilitate their trips across the Atlantic. They also possess a telephone, which I have to disconnect from time to time, owing to the alarming accounts they seem to run up.

As offers of bears arrived by every post at that time, I had to restrict myself to considering only those who were threatened with being put to sleep after years of faithful service and companionship. A lady in Florida asked me to look after her sixty-year-old friend "Stevie" as she was beginning to find him "too much of a responsibility."

He arrived at the theatre one day in an enormous paper parcel. He was a bit threadbare but otherwise pretty endearing. Except for his feet. They smelled *horrible*. I investigated further and found at the bottom of the wrapping a parcel of rotten fish fillets sent by a Florida general store to their head office in New York. I promptly wrote all the authorities to complain that things had come to a pretty pass in a so-called democratic country, when one couldn't even send a Teddy Bear through the post without somebody's attaching stinking denizens of the deep to his poor feet. I did eventually deduce by elimination that the fish had slithered in by error when the Florida postal authorities were checking or repacking the original parcel.

Anyhow, Stevie now sits, merry as a grig, in a chair of honor at the most distinguished publishing house in New York, a fitting end to years of devotion to duty.

Another bear I offered to find a home for in his old age had sat on the shelf of a store in Saco, Maine, for over fifty years. He had given pleasure to generations of customers, but when Ladds Dry Goods Store finally closed its doors he had no home, and Mrs. Euphemia Ladd sent him to me. He was in the pink of condition, though she apologized a lot for the humped back she suspected he had acquired through being on the shelf all those years.

He is a luminous example of the immense charm and stamina of the Teddy Bear who has woven a net for himself to capture hearts round the world.

But when, where, and how did it all begin?

DRAWING
THE LINE
IN MISSISSIPPI

In the Beginning

I've already confessed how shaken I was to find that America claimed the Teddy Bear as its own, and I suppose I was hoping against hope that while I was in the States I would stumble on some new evidence to prove that this was not the case. I knew there was a very small school of thought (British to the core) that maintained the toy was so called after a visit of King Edward VII, then Prince of Wales, to the London Zoo. He took, it is affirmed, a fancy to a Koala bear, and who should blame him?

I did get involved in a certain amount of correspondence supporting this theory. A Mr. Kirby of Little Rock advised me to look at page 5422 of Funk and Wagnall's *Standard Reference Encyclopaedia* where I would find that "the Koala somewhat resembles the toy Teddy Bear which was modeled after it." I took Mr. Kirby's statement on trust as I had already found on page 4194 of the *World Book Encyclopaedia* (1953 edition) that "the Koala is a small Australian animal that is also called the Teddy Bear."

But there are two *principal* contestants for the honor of having made the first Teddy. They are Morris Michtom, who later founded the Ideal Toy Corporation of America, and Margarete Steiff of the German firm of Steiff. There has been great bitterness between the two over the years and there is still a good deal of mystery lurking round the foundations of both their claims.

What *can* be established without the shadow of a doubt is that the whole thing was sparked off by a distinguished cartoonist of the period called Clifford Berryman. For it was he, while working for the *Washington Star*, who drew a picture of Theodore Roosevelt refusing to shoot a small bear cub on a hunting expedition in Mississippi in November 1902.

Roosevelt, the youngest man ever to serve as President, had succeeded the assassinated McKinley in 1901, and a year later had gone south to settle a minor boundary between Mississippi and its neighbor Louisiana by drawing a line between the two states. Berryman, in his simple but historic cartoon, shows the President, gun in hand, turning his back on the small bear and holding up his hand to indicate that he was indeed "Drawing the Line in Mississippi," as the drawing was entitled — a *double entendre* to indicate that he could not bring himself to shoot such a small sitting target.

Berryman's work appeared in newspapers and magazines all over the continent, but I doubt if he realized what an astonishing effect this particular creation would have on the world. The little bear was to become a kind of symbolic signature to many of his political cartoons and provide his President with an endearing and valuable tag which could be (and was) used constantly for publicity purposes.

Somebody who did see the possibilities of the little bear was Morris Michtom, a Russian immigrant, who was the proprietor of a small candy store in Brooklyn which also sold toys, many of them handmade by him or his wife. The moment he saw the drawing he had a brilliant idea. He and his wife cut out the shape of a brown plush bear and stuffed it. The animal had movable limbs and button eyes.

Mr. Michtom put one in the window of his shop, alongside a copy of the Berryman cartoon, and attached a label saying "Teddy's Bear." It was sold almost immediately and replaced by another and so it went on. Mr. M. began to suspect he was on to something good. But did he need authorization from the President of the United States to use his name to promote the article?

Eventually he screwed up enough courage to enclose a sample of the bear with a personal letter he wrote to Mr. Roosevelt, whose Christian name the little bear was destined to carry to immortality. In due course he received a reply from the White House in the President's own handwriting, saying that he couldn't imagine what good his name would be in the stuffed-animal business but that Mr. Michtom was welcome to use it.

In those days it was not possible to patent a trade name, a factor which accounts for the later rush of "Teddy Bears" from every other conceivable quarter.

The enterprising Mr. Michtom went ahead with his plan and took the Presidential letter to a Mr. Schoonmaker, the buyer for Butler Brothers, a large wholesale firm dealing with toys and novelties, and in 1903 this firm took his entire output of Teddy Bears and guaranteed his credit with the local mills which supplied him with the actual plush to construct the animals. Now the Ideal Toy Corporation is among the biggest manufacturers of toys in America. But in those days there was no real hint of the furor the Teddy Bear was going to cause throughout the world, although by the time Mr. Michtom was fully established, there were dozens of firms turning out the little animal all over America and Europe (Sears, Roebuck is believed to have been handling them as early as 1904 and Woolworth's in 1905).

The other main claimant to the invention is the firm of Steiff in Germany, founded in the 1880's by Margarete Steiff, a lady fated by polio to spend most of her life in a wheel chair. Margarete and her sister possessed the first hand-driven sewing machine, which they used to set up back to front so Margarete could turn the wheel with her left hand, which was also somewhat crippled. Yet this remarkable lady was determined to be financially free and independent.

In 1877, when she was thirty, she got very interested in the use of felt, which was then a comparatively new material to the field of dressmaking. One day by chance she found a model of an elephant, and as an experiment, made one out of felt. This she turned into a pincushion and kept for herself. But her friends were delighted by it and she made some for them. In 1880 there were six in existence; by 1885 there were 596; and the next year, 5,066. In 1886 a monkey was added, followed by a donkey, horse, pig, and camel. In 1893 an agent sold her toys for the first time at the famous fair in Leipzig and a catalogue was brought out.

By this time two of her nephews had joined the firm and one of them, Richard, who had studied art in Stuttgart, conceived the idea of making a toy bear with movable joints and head. Bears had always been his favorites at the zoo and he used to spend a great deal of his free time in front of the cages and artificial caves in which they were

25

Theodore Roosevelt and the Teddy Bear

Richard Steiff and early bears from the Steiff kingdom

housed. His aunt, it is reported, was not enthusiastic when she saw the toy; firstly, because she thought it was too large to be popular, and secondly, because it was made of mohair, which was difficult to get in those days. However, the firm decided to have a try and sent Paul Steiff, another nephew (at the time undergoing vocational training in America), one of the bears. He tried to interest various American businessmen in them but they apparently ridiculed the poor creature for its plumpness, heaviness, and general nonconformity.

All this is particularly curious because it was during this year that Mr. Michtom was having his success, on however small a scale, in his Brooklyn store with the animal. The Steiff model, with some slight adjustments, was exhibited at the Leipzig fair in 1903. The buyer of one of the biggest New York import houses took a great fancy to it. I suspect it was F.A.O. Schwarz, but most of their old records have been destroyed and it is impossible to prove this. Anyhow, the representative of whatever firm it was approached the Steiff people, saying that he hadn't been able to find anything new and worthwhile at the fair and that he was looking for something "soft and cuddly." The bear was produced and he put in an order for 3,000 immediately.

It is here that the Steiff story merges inextricably with fiction (or rather the other way round). There had of course been no question of the animal being called "Teddy" because the word would have meant less than nothing to the average German. It is also fairly certain that he was known as "Friend Petz" until quite a good deal later. But in order to substantiate the Steiff claims I must produce the following story from their records.

Before a White House reception in this period, the caterer was having a series of sleepless nights because he couldn't think up a suitable theme for decorating the table. In panic he suddenly took off from Washington to New York, where he found the answer to his problem. He saw, staring at him from a shop window, a little miniature bear from Giengen-on-the Brenz. He bought several and dressed them all as huntsmen (for was not the bride's father a hunter?): some of them carried rifles in their paws and some gold bowls with fishing rods. The guests were apparently highly diverted and one of the President's cronies asked what species of bear they were.

Roosevelt was at a loss for an answer, but a guest (unfortunately, name unspecified) said it was a new species called "Teddy."

It was possibly this incident that started the great boom years for the Steiff family. In 1908 they manufactured a million bears! Margarete Steiff died in 1909, but by then the "Knopf im Ohr" (button in ear) had become famous all over the world as a trademark for her merchandise. Other German firms were meanwhile cashing in (in 1907, for instance, the toymakers of Sonneberg in the Thuringen Mountains were shipping 10,000 bears to America each week).

The Michtom claim to invention is certainly a strong one, though here we run into a series of seemingly inexplicable loose ends. There is, for instance, no trace of the three essential letters which would prove for all time that Morris Michtom was the Teddy Bear's originator.

One is his letter to the President, which understandably was not filed in the White House at the time, but Theodore Roosevelt's reply, giving his permission to use the name of "Teddy," is another kettle of fish altogether. It seems extraordinary that such a valuable document has not been preserved and treasured through the years. Its impact for publicity purposes would have been dynamite and its display (even in photostatic form) on the walls of the New York office of the Ideal Toy Corporation would impress every buyer in the world.

Later there was a letter from Mrs. Theodore Roosevelt to the younger Michtoms to condole with them on the death of their distinguished father, who was mourned in the newspapers throughout America as "The Father of The Teddy Bear." But neither letter has turned up, though Benjamin Michtom remains quite sincerely convinced that his father did indeed invent the "Teddy Bear."

Well, there you are. Take your pick. I am always accused of running with the hare and hunting with the hounds. While I am inclined

Roosevelt Memorabilia

Susan Roosevelt with original Teddy Bear

Campaign button, 1904

HIS INDEPENDENCE DAY

THE CHARLIEBEAR

The President's vacation is progressing finely and bids fair to end in a blaze of glory which is little short of an apotheosis. He has bagged a great deal of game, but none more notable than the big bear of Mississippi, Governor Vardaman. Just what kind of ammunition he used to bring him down the despatches do not state, but the capture is complete. "With all my heart," says the Governor, "I wish Mr. Roosevelt well and am willing to overlook his peculiarities and idiosyncracies. I should like to be friends with him." There's a grizzly landed for sure!

THE BEAR: "DE-LIGHT-ED!"

HERE HE COMES

to support the Michtom story, I also think it highly probable that the Steiffs had brought out a species of "Teddy" at the same time, if not before. But I bet the Russians were manufacturing toy replicas of their national animal centuries before *either* of them.

Let's just admit that whether it was a he or a she, an American, a German, a Russian, or an Englishman who first caught the magic in his hand, children and grownups of all ages the world over owe him an awful lot.

Immune to all the controversy it had unwittingly stirred up, Berryman's Teddy Bear continued to appear for many years, and rather like Hirschfield's "Nina" in the *New York Times* and elsewhere, became an integral part of the design. In October 1907 another Presidential bear hunt was the inspiration for another very successful drawing. Called "The President Dreams of a Successful Hunt" it shows him with one foot resting on a dead bear (BAD TRUSTS). Tied to his waist by a belt marked RESTRAINT is another bear, live but cowering (GOOD TRUSTS).

In the background is the original Teddy Bear, happy as a clam, carrying a sackful of bears.

The symbol was still being used in 1917, when on the eve of America's entering World War I, Mr. Berryman drew a cartoon of which there is no trace of publication but which says on the back of the original drawing: "Given to my father John Paul Ernest." It shows the President of the United States (Woodrow Wilson) with one of his hands clutching a scroll titled "Strenuous American Policy" and the other grasping Uncle Sam, who is sitting gloomily at a desk, surrounded by lurid posters saying things like "Hun Atrocities in Belgium," "Lusitania Sinking," and "Red Cross Hospitals Attacked by German Airmen." Uncle Sam is protesting, "I fear I've waited too long," but Wilson, firm behind his pince-nez, says, "It's NEVER too late to start RIGHT." In the background Teddy Bear stands coyly but bravely holding the American flag.

Although Teddy was appearing in print from 1902 in the form of drawings, he doesn't appear to have crashed any other medium. In May 1906 the first advertisement for Teddy Bears seems to have been presented to the general public. This was in the toy trade magazine *Playthings* and read: "This is Bruin's Day . . . The American line of jointed plush bears is the real thing. Polar Bear, Cinnamon Bear, Grizzly Bear. Baker and Bigler sole manufacturers." Note that there is still no mention of the magic word "Teddy," though the patriotic emphasis in the ad suggests that foreign bears had already seriously invaded the market.

It wasn't until 1906 that *Playthings* was full of references to the newcomer on the toy market. That year Kahn and Mossbacher, manufacturers of dolls' outfits, were urging customers to "make our happiest hit your happiest hit! Everything for the Teddy Boy and Teddy Girl!" Ferguson, an early toy pioneer, offered Teddy in a baseball suit, a turtle-necked sweater, overalls and even Rough Rider uniform. The Keystone Novelty Company was willing to sell "Bears fully equal to the finest imported" — which again shows that the home producers were determined to lead in the bear market.

Round about this time sales were helped immeasurably by the great success of a series of books about two characters called "The Roosevelt Bears." A writer and illustrator called Paul Piper, who wrote under the name of Seymour Eaton, created "Teddy G" (Good) and "Teddy B" (Bad), whose antics swept the nation. A manufacturer called E. J. Horsman appears to have been the first actually to *call* his bears "Teddies" when advertising his wares in *Playthings*. In fact, he put "Teddy's," which he amended to "Teddy Bears" in November 1906 when catering for the latest fad to use the animals, in the form of side lamps for cars. He was obviously not all that patriotic, as we find him in December 1906 pushing "Imported Teddy Bears — best quality with voice $4.50 to $72 a dozen — and also DOMESTIC TEDDY BEARS with voice, Horsman's extra quality $9 to $36 a dozen."

Although the craze for Teddy Bears greatly increased the sale of all kinds of stuffed animals, there is no doubt that it was only the

JUNE 22D 1910

MELON

POTAGE DE SANTÉ

SAUMON CASCAPEDIA
SAUCE MOUSSELINE

SELLE D'AGNEAU DE PRINTEMPS
POMMES CASSEROLE
CHAMPIGNONS AU BEURRE LIÉ

ASPERGES BROOKDALE

SUPRÊME DE PINTADE NIMROD
HARICOTS DE LIMA ET PIMENTS DOUX

JAMBON DE VIRGINIE FARCI
SALADE TROPHY

GLACES AUX FRAMBOISES, POLONNAISE
GATEAUX   FRUITS
CAFÉ
CHAMPAGNE
LOUIS ROEDERER 1900

PRESENTED BY J. J. VAN ALEN, ESQ.
AND CLARENCE H. MACKAY, ESQ.
PRESENTED BY LEWIS S. THOMPSON, ESQ.

Menu used at dinner for Theodore Roosevelt

HOW THE BEARS REACHED NEW YORK

The story tells of their further jaunt
  And of TEDDY–G at a restaurant;
    How he missed his train and lost his mate;
    For TEDDY–B had risen late;
  And the jolly crowds the bears to greet
To cheer them all along the street

As they rode from station to Common green
In Boston town like king or queen;
And of the home on Beacon Hill
Where Priscilla Alden and her brother Will
Entertained them gladly days and nights
While they were seeing the Boston sights.

But the things they did in Boston town
Are done in picture and written down
In Volume One by Teddy's paw,
The jolliest book you ever saw.
It tells how they captured Bunker Hill
And worked like soldiers with stubborn will;
And how they got lost in Boston squares
Where criss-cross streets run everywheres;

And the time they had at Plymouth Rock
When trying to make forefathers talk;
And the auto ride to Lexington
Which nearly cost them all their fun,
For TEDDY–G would chauffeur be
And he ran that car like sixty-three;
It didn't run; he made it sail
And landed himself and his mate in jail.

Presidentially-inspired toy that caused so much fierce competition among toymakers and stores alike.

The Tingue Manufacturing Company of Seymour, Connecticut, was apparently using the wool of four thousand goats per week. These animals were now immensely valuable: a good buck (if I may use the phrase) fetched as much as a thousand ditto.

1907 saw the creation of the Bruin Manufacturing Company. The Fast Black Skirt Company rather surprisingly turned out "Electric Bright-Eye Teddy Bears — Shake the Right Paw, Eyes Light Up White or Red. Also Thirty-six-Inch Bear for Autos." Leo Shlesinger offered Teddy Bear pails and Teddy Bear tea sets, while the Lloyd Manufacturing Company of Menominee, Michigan, announced: "The Best Selling Novelty of the Year," which turned out to be Teddy Bear carts and cages. Pedal cars were advertised with bears driving them; a Teddy Bear hammock was followed by a Teddy Bear squeeze ball; there were Teddy Bear targets, paper dolls, party games, penny banks, blocks, wagons, scarf pins, rubber stamps, water pistols, postcards, candy boxes, cotillion favors, balloons, bags, briefcases (of plush, natch!), books, card games, shoo-flies, rocking horses, muzzles, and leashes. Strauss, the self-designated "Toy King," made a "self-whistling Teddy Bear." There were Tumbling Teddies and even one with a doll's face, which seems about as far as you can go.

Certainly the whole thing was going *too* far for some people. There was, for instance, a Michigan priest who denounced the Teddy Bear as destroying all instincts of motherhood and leading to race suicide. A Mrs. Harry Hastings of New York answered this by saying: "Nonsense! I think they are the cutest, dearest, best-behaved little visitors we've ever entertained. I draw the line on their going to church, however."

There were other replies to the irate clergyman. A baby-carriage merchant announced that "Teddy Bears may be a menace to motherhood in Michigan but we are selling more baby barouches than ever before!" And a woman on Sullivan Street in New York gathered ten of her fifteen children around her and said (and I quote the newspaper verbatim):

"Tiddy Bears, is it? An' sure more than half the kiddies on the block have thim little growlers, an' I don't see any signs av race Soorside in this neighborhood. Oi think that afther wan or two more come along to give me a noice dacint family to bring up, Oi'll be gittin' Danny to git me a noice big Tiddy to kape in the house."

Many people worried over another aspect of the craze: the decline in the popularity of dolls. A poem, published in a magazine called *St. Nicholas*, was entitled "The Days of Long Ago" and was written by a minor poet of the period (I use the word "minor" in its strictest sense, for Miss Marion Lincoln Hussey, the author, was only nine years old at the time):

> *In the long ago I was once brand new,*
> *With silk and satin and lace.*
> *My coat was of velvet, my hat of real felt,*
> *And oh, I moved with such grace.*

After a few more lines of boastful reminiscence by this allegedly lovely doll, the poem ends:

> *But no, oh, 'tis said that I am disgraced*
> *By a modern Teddy Bear.*

"It is enough to make a perfect lady of a doll mad," a magazine editor wrote. "The dear little girls, who have always cried for dolls at Christmas, are this year crying for Teddy Bears, and dolls are left on the shelf to cry the paint off their pretty cheeks because of the neglect."

And *still* some toy people would not believe the craze would last! In October of 1907 one retailer claimed, without a sign of a wink, that "bears are on their last legs." A month later, however, he had to admit "that crazy bear is as popular as ever."

And indeed he spread to all fields. The circus at Madison Square

37

Oh Joy! Wonderful

20-Inch

$1.75 Teddy Bear

This pleasant looking bear is made of good quality cinnamon color plush. Fully jointed, glass eyes. We offer this serviceable toy at a very low price. Shipping weight, 2½ pounds.

48D3201—Price only $1.75

39

59c

10-Inch Teddy Bear

We have endeavored to give the little tots the best bear we could procure at a low price. Made of good quality cinnnamon color plush. Has natural looking eyes, Head, arms and legs are jointed. Ship. wt., ¾ lb.

48D3178— **59c** Price ....

5

Toys for Girl or Boy

The Funny Climbing Monkey

The monkey actually climbs the string, moving its arms and legs in a very funny manner. The children will scream with laughter when they see how lifelike it is. Made of metal, neatly decorated in colors. Length, 8 inches. Ship., wt., 6 oz.

48D2051—Each .. **39c**

11-Inch Teddy Bear with Voice

$1.10

Glass eyes. Made of good grade long pile brown color plush, fully jointed. This is the cutest little bear and will make many youngsters' hearts leap with joy. A high-grade bear at a medium price. Ship. wt., ½ lb.

48D3247— Price, only **$1.10**

16-Inch Teddy Bear $1.48

For a good sized bear, this one will bring happiness to the children. Made of good quality plush, cinnamon color. Head, arms and legs are jointed. Shipping weight, 1¼ pounds.

48D3199 —

Price **$1.48**

dressed some of its clowns and even trick dogs as Teddy Bears. And in certain vaudeville shows of the day the chorus girls came out dressed as them. In the "New Operatic Absurdity" called *The Toymakers*, there was a song entitled "There's Nothing Else But Teddy," in which a Miss Grace Lavelle was accompanied by four young ladies hideously disguised in bear costumes that must have been stifling.

Then there was the popular joke of the period: "If Theodore is President of the United States with his clothes on, what is he with his clothes off? Answer: "TEDDY BARE." The joke had a British counterpart as well: Lily Langtry, the Jersey Lily and King Edward VII's great and good friend, was said to prefer her Teddy Bare. But the Teddy Bear craze was never as frenzied in Great Britain as in the States, where, between 1907 and 1911, everyone was positively Teddy Bear mad. In Minneapolis, the Dayton Dry Goods Company had a "Live Teddy Bear" to welcome the children every afternoon at four-thirty. One of the big stores in Philadelphia, for the opening of the baseball season, had a window display of the ballpark with Teddy Bears in the uniforms of the Athletics and Phillies, in which grandstand and bleachers were full of cheering bears. In one clothing emporium, Teddies were dressed in really gorgeous gowns of velvet and lace. And wearing jewels. Lawks! Luckily, to balance things out, other bears wore Columbia, Yale, and Princeton football uniforms and carried footballs.

Then there is the legendary story of the blue-ribbon bulldog (worth $2,000 according to its New Orleans owner) which had been brought up with a bear cub which, alas, died suddenly. The dog lost its spirit, its appetite, and finally even its desire to live. One day, on the way to the vet, the dog saw a Teddy Bear in a window, approximately the same size and color as his old friend. Pressing his nose against the pane, he refused to trot on. His owner bought the Teddy Bear and the bulldog regained his spirit, put on weight, and loved life once more. He carried the Teddy tenderly in his mouth wherever he went, poked the bear's nose in his dish of food at mealtimes, and slept on top of him at night (which I can't think was wildly comfortable for poor Teddy).

The craze was at its height in 1909, when Theodore Roosevelt left the Presidency. Since that hunting expedition in Mississippi, where the whole thing had started, he had served out three years of McKinley's second term and four of his own. He had busted trusts, started digging the Panama Canal, and mediated in the Russo-Japanese war; yet to millions he will be known best for his participation in the birth of the Teddy Bear.

And what of the original animal, made with such perspicacity by the candy-store owner in Brooklyn, Morris Michtom? As late as June 19, 1963, there is a letter (fortunately extant) to Benjamin Michtom from Mrs. Kermit Roosevelt, saying that her children still didn't want to part with it, but in fact he now rests in the Smithsonian Institution. Theodore Roosevelt's great-grandchild was photographed with the original Teddy (in person) on the sixtieth anniversary of his birth.

Children today probably can't believe that the toy is comparatively that new and hasn't been around forever. But as you will see from the following pages, Teddy's appeal for young and old has never faltered, and though he is younger, he is just as stable an institution as Father Christmas. And, I fancy, just as indestructible.

Little Bear Lost

One thing I want to make clear at the outset: though only a few of my correspondents have expressed a desire to remain anonymous, I trust that the majority won't mind if I don't give their names—it's a question of monotony and this sort of name-dropping is apt to lose any point and just confuse everyone—*but* the Bears themselves who have sent in their own contributions will receive full acknowledgement, as I know from bitter experience that they are very touchy about this sort of thing.

Owing to the fact that I've been able to expose my enormous face on the television screens of only the United States and Great Britain, practically all the information has come in from these two countries and really frightfully little from countries like Tibet or Lapland. Furthermore, it is a disquieting but proven fact that over six times as many serious letters have been received from American bear owners as light-hearted ones, whereas from Great Britain it's roughly the reverse.

This is not the moment to discuss the passion for self-analysis in America, but I do think the British are inclined to take everything more flippantly, an attitude which has doubtless landed us in our present predicament. As some cynic so aptly put it, we are gradually sinking giggling into the ocean.

All the incoming mail has had one thing in common. The writers have not only had their lives affected by contact with Teddy Bears, but always for the better. No one has reviled the little creatures or described them as pernicious, useless, or unhealthy, and not one person has intimated that they thought I was crazy or even just eccentric to be carrying on about them the way I do. In fact, ninety-five percent

43

of the correspondents treated the whole thing in a completely adult way, even when looking at it through a child's eyes. I'm not so sure about the ladies who married gentlemen because they looked like Teddy Bears, but we'll deal with that situation later.

A lot of parents seem to have realized the extent of the involvement of children with their toys and the dangers of tampering with any such relationship, so I think I'll start with this aspect:

"To children, Teddy Bears to whom they become attached over many years are much more than inanimate objects, and an ill-advised and abrupt separation may have as serious an emotional effect as the death of a close friend." So wrote a lady from New Jersey, and she certainly hit the nail on top of its not wildly attractive head.

An anonymous British-born gent, now living in America, told me that he hadn't spoken to either of his parents for twenty-five years because they had thrown his Teddy into the fire when he was seven. I mean the boy was seven. The deceased was five. His father had done the dreadful deed himself, egged on apparently by his mother. The effect of this incident on the boy was such that he saved up all his pennies, and when he was eight, bought a new bear. This he carefully and wisely kept from his parents, and the Teddy survived to accompany his owner through his studies at Oxford University and doubtless assisted him in achieving his doctorate. Subsequently they marched gallantly together through the German lines toward the end of World War II.

Not all those deprived were so resilient or so resourceful, however, and a lady from New Hampshire came out with the blunt confession that losing her Teddy at the age of seven was "as traumatic as losing my parents." This is a particularly poignant admission as it was exactly what had already happened to her. After their deaths the estate was settled by some idiots who bandied about such nonsense as "No child of your age should have such an infantile toy," ending in the inevitable separation. As she had been an only child, she regarded the bear not merely as a confidante and friend but as the sole survivor of her family. You can imagine her inconsolable grief at losing the one thing which had shared her life up till then. At a highly impressionable age she found herself "shut off entirely from her former world" and resenting it deeply.

It is in emergencies like this that, failing the comfort which a sensitive adult can provide, you feel the need for a beloved object. Obviously you can do without constant moral support, but it's nice to know that it's on tap, even if it's lying in a toy cupboard or a rather inaccessible closet—on a stand-by call, often neglected for months, even years.

As in the case of a young gentleman from Blassevale, who had to all intents and purposes discarded his Teddy in favor of a dog. I say "to all intents and purposes" because the bear had been placed high on a dresser and not touched or moved in years, though we can hope that he had at least been dusted. However, four years after the dog came into the boy's life, it was killed. On the night following the tragedy, when adopted mother went to tuck the little boy in, there was Teddy back in bed, snuggled up to his friend.

On the other hand, exactly the opposite situation arose in the home of Mrs. Marty Simmons, who had a bear called Georgie. He suffered an untimely end when her dog ate up his insides. She does report that the dog got very sick, but as she points out, "that didn't help Georgie much." Mrs. Simmons doesn't say whether the bear was a Georgie Boy or a Georgie Girl.

Lady bears are rare, and one of the few who has come to my notice is a sort of sexual misfit. She belongs to an obviously very nice couple who live in Santa Barbara. Although the legal name is Theodora and female clothes are worn, *she* is only referred to as "he," which must be not a little confusing to the poor little blighter. But this has never been much of a problem to *his* owners, though in *her* eagerness to make *him* more socially acceptable, Mrs. Fenton was inspired to rip out "the grouchy wild bear mouth" and sew on a smile. It paid dividends, this seemingly violent act, because years later, when the Fentons had to flee a raging brush fire threatening their home, the only things they took with them were the clothes on their backs, an antique

Treasured bears

candelabra, some favorite recipes and Teddy (rescued from a knitting bag), "whose unwavering smile incited courage in all of us."

Perhaps the most stark letter I have had on this aspect came from a lady whose beloved brother kept a Teddy as his constant companion. Fifty years ago he loved him through thick and thin, and even when a far too playful playmate took the bear home, shaved his head and trimmed his ears a bit, it didn't seem to worry him all that much. But years later he married a woman who didn't understand about Teddies and was a careless mover as well. The inevitable happened: one day she left Teddy behind, to be lost forever. The rot set in and "the three-martini businessmen's lunch, long waits in airports, and too-long cocktail hours before dinner—my brother became an alcoholic and two years afterwards a well-placed pistol shot ended it all."

Pretty dramatic, eh?

Brothers seem very often to have been the villains of the piece, as in the case of the lady from Schenectady who went visiting her relations in the South, with her brother, when she was four years old. They were accompanied by their parents, but she was palmed off on some slightly older cousins, who tended to gang up on her, assisted by her brother. One of the things the little beasts thought up was to bury her Teddy Bear; they had convinced her, you see, that she was too big to have one. They swore her to secrecy, assuring her that they would treat her like one of them (i.e., grownup) if she would go along with their scheme.

So she had to watch her beloved friend being packed into a coffin and put underground. Her innate shyness was such that she was unable to tell anyone about this horrible experience, but many years later she dug up the spot. The only recognizable signs were the poor little fellow's shoe-button eyes. The lasting effect of the affair on the lady may be gauged by what she told me at the end of the story. "I have always been one to take myself seriously. Very. I am a strict moralist and overresponsible, taking on burdens I could evade. I wonder if the deprivation of my Teddy had anything to do with it. I mean, making me this sort of person."

I think it probably had. But what kind of consequences attend even more brutal and senseless examples of children's cruelty! A six-year-old Teddy owner was forced to watch his brother, curious to know what was going on inside the animal, take it to the basement and chop it up with an ax. Ugh!

I know one lady who will never forget what her brother did to her bear. Now in her sixties, she is haunted by the memory. She had a lovely big white Teddy and her brother had a smaller brown one. One day she couldn't find hers anywhere, and while she was looking for it, her mother started sniffing and wondering what could be burning. There wasn't a sign of the brother around, and when her mother opened the oven, in which she was baking, there was Teddy, burned almost to a cinder, with all his lovely white hair singed.

If the threat of jealous brothers and friends to Teddy Bears weren't enough, it's astonishing how careless their very owners can be. Out of 400,000 articles lost on London Transport vehicles every year, about 250 are Teddy Bears. I am glad to report that practically all are claimed, for nothing is sadder than a little bear lost.

Incidentally, a family of five go to the church of Santa Maria Sopra Minerva every time they are in Rome to give thanks at Saint Anthony's altar for the recovery in that church of a Teddy Bear they lost some years ago.

But not every separation has as happy an ending. I have a great friend who had to watch his beloved animal swept away by a flood tide which had encircled his house. Although he was thirteen he couldn't swim and his father had forcibly to hold him back from trying to rescue his bear.

Adults can be caused just as much distress as children by the loss of a toy. Why, only the other day there was an advertisement in the Personal Columns of *The Times* which read quite simply: "Lost in Cadogan Square Gardens a tired but much loved Teddy Bear." Freddie, the pop singer of Freddie and the Dreamers, was inconsolable when he lost his, and Princess Alexandra of Kent took it very badly when she mislaid hers during a good-will tour of the Far East in December 1961.

A bare necessity in every home

Both the Burmese Army and the R.A.F. had to confess failure after massive hunts near the Irrawaddy River.

And so did the searchers for Inky, a black Teddy Bear belonging to Cynthia Hobart.* There was a newspaper story about forty years ago which was headlined:

HAS ANYBODY SEEN A TEDDY BEAR?

Cynthia, five, and bereaved of her best-beloved companion since last Wednesday, tearfully awaits news of him today.

It is possible that one might have seen Inky without recognizing his value. Here is a detailed description of him issued by Cynthia herself:

"His eyes were worsted cause the others, real ones you know, came out. One ear got chewed. And his hair was comin' off, cause, you see, I washed him every day. He'd had a bath and powder on him, cause you see, we were goin' to Coney Island."

It was at the very start of this festive expedition that Inky was lost. He was riding in a sandpail carried by his little mother and the grownup theory is that he must have fallen out. Cynthia thinks he may have done it on purpose, just for fun. She explains that he was fond of mischief.

But she thinks he has teased her enough now and she wants him home. Every night when she is ready to go to bed she cries, because Inky always slept with her. And during the day she refuses to leave the house, because she thinks the telephone might ring with news of him or somebody might ring with news of him or somebody might bring him back to her.

She knows that an "agony" advertisement for Inky was inserted right between the notice of a large jewel loss and that of a bond disappearance in a New York paper, and

*Cynthia Hobart, without Inky alas, grew up to become a distinguished writer. Her best-known work perhaps is *The Natives Are Restless*, about life in Southern California.

she believes somebody may bring the lost toy home again.

The child has literally dozens of dolls in her home at 150 Clinton Street, Brooklyn, dolls of wax, bisque and cloth. In a room almost entirely given over to them—but she refuses to play with any of them. There's another Teddy Bear too, but—"They're not Inky," she says, sadly, and the big tears start from her brown eyes and roll right down her rosy cheeks. The Coney Island expedition was, of course, given up entirely, and not five minutes after the disappearance was discovered, fifty men were hunting along Joralemon Street, where the tragedy is thought to have occurred, but there was no trace of Inky.

While Cynthia slept the other day, hair like Inky's was put on another doll and the doll was laid beside her pillow, so she might see it when she awoke. Cynthia looked at the doll, then at her mother.

"It's a nice doll, but I don't feel like playin'—till Inky comes home," she said gently.

"He'll come back," she asserted confidently today. "Once before he did—but oh" and here the tears started again—"I wish he'd hurry!"

The Hon. Alison Ruthven and her bear Daddy Gruff (1906)

On the Couch

Teddy, Teddy, you're my sweetheart true.
You're never bold
You never scold
You all my troubles share.
What would I do without you dear
Old Teddy Teddy Bear.

Dr. Joshua Bierer, medical director of the Institute of Social Psychiatry in London, is a firm believer in the powers of the Teddy Bear. He says it is all to do with touch ("they are soft and warm and feel nice") and that most people have within them a love of animals and the Teddy Bear is the only nondangerous animal in the nursery. "Teddies," he adds, "are father figures. To children they represent goodness, benevolence, kindliness. Parents who replace this cozy unharmful toy are a menace."

Parents and others are very arbitrary in deciding when a child should stop having his or her Teddy Bear around. My mother thought sixteen was about the right time. I still think she was wrong and I'm sure Theodore agrees with me.

One Pittsburgh lady was even more ruthless in the matter of her son's Teddy, a huge blue bear called Pooh, whom she removed from his bed when he was nearly fourteen and five-foot-two. She softened the blow by offering to take care of him herself, but she hasn't issued any statement as to his reaction. The fact that she herself (five-foot-ten and a hundred and fifty pounds) was going to bed with a yellow and lavender rabbit was, she asserts defiantly, "totally different." Anyhow, now she has the best of both possible worlds, as Pooh has retired to a chair in her bedroom from which he watches her out of his one pink eye as she makes the bed. I suspect, a bit reproachfully.

Then there is the frightfully tricky problem of replacing a decrepit but loved bear with a new one. It is astonishing how some parents can be so snobbish and short-sighted. They actually *do* look down on a family with a Teddy who is not in the absolute pink of condition. After all, the Acropolis and the Pyramids aren't in a state of perfect preservation and yet people have been known to think quite highly of them. What this type of parent doesn't seem to realize is that children dread Change in any form. It's simply no use trying to foist a brand-new object of possible affection on them when they are still devoted to their old friends, be they dolls, blankets, or bears. I have countless examples of attempted substitution but in all cases the experiment has failed.

Is it any wonder? Most head-shrinkers to whom I have talked see Teddy as a bridging object, a symbol used by people of all ages to recapture infant security in the face of frightening new situations. Some of them, unlike Dr. Bierer, see him as a mother figure because he is the first warm cuddly object that registers with a baby.

Nor is that the only reason for discouraging the weaning of a child from a beloved toy. Owners, you know, assume all sorts of guilt for whatever mishaps may befall their toys. I know of a young Brooklyn lady who was forced to give up her Teddy at the age of eight. She refused to throw him into the garbage can. As a sort of compromise, he was deposited in the basement. A year later she sought refuge beside him after a terrible scolding.

Sometimes, however, there are high-minded reasons for passing on a treasured bear: there are many cases of owners surrendering them (I suspect under great pressure) for a good cause like a war. What am I saying? *Good* cause? But you know what I mean. The animals are raffled off and the money made is put aside to buy soldiers' comforts, etc. (I imagine the "etc." includes small Teddy Bears to comfort them). And similar steps are taken to improve the lot of underprivileged children; I know that Lady Heald sends Teddy Bears direct to Hong Kong to comfort deprived mites.

Short of parting with them for humanitarian reasons, most of us arctophilists would rather hang on to our bears than anything—in whatever condition they are. Unless they have been badly injured. I

THE TEDDY BEAR

MARCH
AND
TWO STEP

by
ALBERT A.
WILLIAMS.

PUBLISHED BY
ALBERT A. WILLIAMS
121 ST JOHN STREET
NEW HAVEN, CONN.

am thinking in particular of a Teddy whose ears were chewed off by an overenthusiastic puppy, a newcomer to the household. Although the bear's owner was fourteen years old she cried as if one of the family had died. She had the bear put away because she couldn't face seeing his injuries. The mother of the girl comments rather sadly: "It has always seemed strange to me that Nancy was not angry with the dog for damaging the bear, but with me for allowing it, and of course I didn't see what he was doing until it was done."

Of course, in emotional circumstances it is very difficult to know where the guilt lies. It's fascinating to discover how many children will deliberately take it out on their toys for some crime they themselves have committed. A little chap who used to live in Pennsylvania dunked Squeaky, his Teddy Bear, into a can of paint for reasons unspecified. Naturally the dunkee stopped squeaking and in fact had to be thrown away. A substitute was found. Yet instead of being delighted with what was tactfully referred to as "Squeaky's Brother," the lad kept hitting him and even pulling his eyes out. It wasn't for some time that anyone could see his motives. Then it suddenly became clear. He was punishing the new addition to the family as he would have punished himself for what he had done to Squeaky. He eventually threw a rock at a squirrel and thought he'd killed it. After this appalling behavior he wouldn't be comforted. "I know I won't go to heaven," he said tearfully. "I killed Squeaky and a baby 'quirrel." I can't think he can ever have been a frightfully easy child to cope with. My only hope is that he has settled down now to a less destructive way of life.

As has a distinguished newspaper gentleman I know who confessed to me that he used to treat his Teddy Bear as a whipping boy — literally. The animal was called Teddles and had a squeak in his navel. He also had a head which swiveled three hundred and sixty degrees. The fact that he was an acknowledged member of the family didn't prevent my friend from booting him savagely, throwing him against the wall and out of bed onto the floor. This kind of beastliness affected the little horror between the ages of five and seven; afterwards he would be overcome by remorse and lavish cuddles on Teddles.

There is a rather charming postscript to this little tale. My friend assures me that in all his adult life he has never felt the slightest inclination to raise a fist to another human being.

Of course, the great advantage of having a loyal friend who can't answer back is that you can blame him for anything and he can't deny it. "Teddy did it" is a phrase which must have passed through thousands of tiny lips the moment a valuable piece of china was swept to the floor or a door slammed in somebody's face. I know a young gentleman from Boston who went on using his bear as a shield for his iniquities for so long that his parents finally sent him to a psychiatrist.

It is very difficult to follow all the workings of a child's mind anyway, but when imagination itself runs riot, it is well-nigh impossible. But we know that the fear of disapproval or punishment is never far away and it's always nice to have a furry friend around so that there is at least one other person who can share any unpleasantness that may crop up.

Therefore, it's not too surprising that non-owners of Teddy Bears are envious of others' luck. Cousins in both these categories seem to breed special trouble. A young lady called Eth possessed a Teddy Bear nicknamed "The Perfessor." Her small male cousin coveted him desperately and one day grabbed him from her. He was astounded at what happened then: "My hair was pulled and tiny but lethal fingernails raked my cheek. Chivalry be damned! I smacked her but good. And then a heavy hand smote me. Her adoring grandpa had watched the whole scene and my villainy was reported, resulting in subsequent corporal punishment at home. I never asked again for a Teddy Bear, I never again struck a female, and today I am a vile-tempered neurotic old bachelor."

Would he have been a happier man if he had had a Teddy Bear of his own? Well, you know what my answer would be.

Children are hooked on their Teddies and a lot of American kids find it difficult to know when to stop taking their chums to summer camp. I heard a rather touching tale of a small fellow who carefully tried to bridge the gap. At the age of seven he won the award of "Best

It's his bear, Mr. Photographer

Camper." The following year he asked his mother to make a suit for his Teddy Bear on which he wanted to display the award. "The truth was," reported his observant mother, "he realized that having a Teddy in camp might not be considered quite manly. By giving Teddy the award he thought he might continue the relationship he had not outgrown, at the same time avoiding the teasing expected. As far as we can tell it worked."

Perhaps the most sentimental example of self-sacrifice was that of a young lady from Long Island. Her bear was called Flat Ted (because he had attained a completely smooth state after years of being "hugged, coddled and snuggled"). Devoted though she was to him, she let her father take him on his business trips for companionship. He was an uncomplaining and hardy passenger, but after years of joint motoring her father died, and his daughter made a startling decision. She insisted that Flat Ted be buried near her father's heart "to remind him always of me." She added: "I love and miss them very much."

But I meant to end this chapter on a cheerful note. All right! Here is some jazzy aristocratic news about Teddies. Lady Beatty took one on her honeymoon. Lady Shrewsbury used to keep one on her bed; it's rumored that Viscount Furness still does. And: one of millionaire Paul Getty's ex-wives has one constructed out of mink — hoop-la!

The Therapeutic Powers of Edward Bear

Poor Teddy Bear is awful bad, he tore his head today.
It's baby's fault, but then I think boys are rough when they play.
Nurse got her needle and some silk, and sewed the hole up quick,
But when the sawdust tumbled out, I cried till I was sick;
I'm glad that I was sick, because, when nurse took baby out,
I stayed indoors alone with Ted, and carried him about.

I'm sparing you the chorus of "The Sick Teddy Bear" as written by Daisy McGeogh because I doubt if you could take it so early on in a new chapter.

But the above excerpt is sufficient for you to realize that there are clearly two patients involved, one a small girl and the other a stuffed animal. This isn't so very odd. I've received many letters giving examples of shared ill-health.

"When I was five years old I was given a beautiful Teddy just before I had to undergo a serious abdominal operation. The surgeon, one of the famous Mixter brothers, shaved Teddy's abdomen and with red ink made a scar similar to my own." So wrote Mrs. Eleanor Johnson, and she, like so many of my correspondents, seems to have noticed far more how their Teddies were treated than how much pain they themselves were undergoing.

Mrs. Johnson was fortunate in being allowed the companionship of her friend: some hospitals on both sides of the Atlantic won't allow this for hygienic reasons. And a pity that is, since a child in distress will naturally turn to his constant friend for moral support; being deprived of him at a critical moment may lead to a lot of distress and confusion.

"Theodore P. Bear" was a wailing noise set up by a four-year-old having his tonsils and adenoids out, after an overzealous nurse had removed his Teddy. The words meant nothing to her but everything to the little boy.

One Tennessee tonsilitis sufferer took his Bermuda-born bear to a naval hospital. They were together up to the moment the anesthetic was administered. On returning to consciousness, he found himself alone. He had apparently got sick all over his friend and that was that. The boy searched everywhere for him without success and remains to this day inconsolable.

Even if, after the operation, the Teddy that so proudly you hailed is still there, it is essential not to let him out of your sight. Hospitals are funny places and not like home at all. I know one boy, in bed with rheumatic fever, who felt his companion was not getting enough exercise and should be allowed out for walks. He lowered him carefully from the window when no one was looking. One awful day, while the bear was out for his daily stroll, the little boy felt the string go light. He hauled it up to find that some horrible bear-fancier had taken advantage of the situation and made off with his Teddy.

Somebody who realized the importance of a child's having a friend with him in the hospital was Russell McLean, who became known throughout America as "The Teddy Bear Man." He has been plagued all his life with illness and in fact spent much of his childhood in a hospital bed. He remembered what the loneliness there was like and decided to do something about it. Over twenty years ago he approached a radio station in his native Ohio and by good luck found a sympathetic listener in Miss Easter Straker, a well-known local broadcaster. He told her his dream: to buy Teddy Bears and leave them at both of the big hospitals in Lima, Ohio — to be presented to all children the first night they were left there, alone and terrified, by their parents.

Miss Straker thought the idea splendid; the problem was how to finance it. Then the determined Mr. McLean had a brilliant idea. At that time Ohio had a three percent sales tax and each retailer gave you a sales-tax stamp when you bought an item. To help make their tax more palatable, the state redeemed these stamps at one percent of their face value for charitable organizations. Mr. McLean thought that the project might be financed this way. His scheme was enormously successful—people sent in their stamps by the thousands and he and his wife dealt with them themselves.

Ultimately the state dropped the tax-stamp plan but by that time the project was well established and the money kept rolling in from other sources. Miss Straker has a daily TV show on which children appear and sit on a Birthday Chair. It has become a sort of ritual that the birthday child gives a dollar to the Teddy Bear Man. At Christmas there is a special drive and thousands of dollars are raised regularly through direct solicitation of viewers. Mr. McLean ran the whole thing from his own home until the death of his wife. And even after his own health failed to the point where he had to retire to a nursing home, he continued in his work. He achieved his great ambition when he presented his fifty-thousandth Teddy Bear. Soon after this he had to give up active participation but a club called the Greater Lima Jaycees stepped in and took over. They have already won a State Award for their work. Miss Straker, who still helps with the fund-raising, writes movingly of an early incident:

> *I went out to the hospital one day with Mr. McLean and we found a little boy there who had been hit by a car. For several days he would not open his left eye. The doctors felt there was nothing wrong, but no one could coax him. His mother and father were in the room when we came in. Mr. McLean took a Teddy Bear and tucked it into the crook of the little boy's left arm. He reached up with his hand to see what it was, then he began to pat it faster and faster, and then his left eye opened so he could see his bear, and all was well.*

Miss Straker goes on to say:

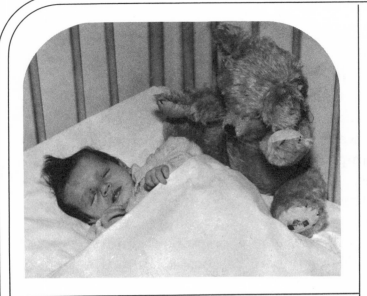

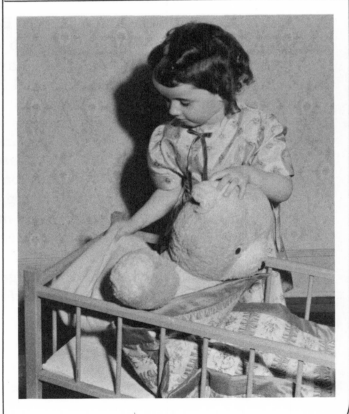

The bear's place in the nursery

Comforter and friend

We get letters, with money enclosed, from parents who didn't take their children home but did take the much-cherished Teddy Bear and still have it. We have second-generation children now and I'm convinced that there isn't a child in Ohio who doesn't expect his Teddy when he gets to the hospital. In fact, parents have told me that getting the child to go there is not particularly difficult because they want a stuffed toy. We are considering this year at Christmas time having a display of the Teddy Bears which sixty thousand youngsters have now received. Only one of Mr. McLean's dreams has not come true. He has earnestly prayed that his plan would be adopted in other parts of the country as well. We hope so too. Our Teddy Bear Man was a dear, dear man — one of God's saints.

Mr. McLean recalled cases of children who refused to eat or even speak until presented with the cuddly animals. Out of the thousands of grateful letters he received, I must quote a few:

We are a family of nine children and would like to express our thanks for four Teddy Bears we have received so far. When our daughter Doris was not expected to live, she still clutched her Teddy during the few minutes she was conscious. Well, our miracle girl lived and we will never forget her Teddy Bear.

A skeptical parent wrote:

I didn't think much of your project at first. I thought all those children already have a favorite toy. What could a new little Teddy do? Then I found out. *Our four-year-old child had an accident and was completely terrified at finding herself hospitalized. Then came that little Teddy at a time when nothing else would have done. Our girl is now grownup but she still has that Teddy.*

And from another parent:

My daughter was suddenly desperately ill. I never thought to grab up a toy for her until she was handed a

66

Teddy from you. She immediately thought only of it and hugged it almost to pieces while the doctor worked on her.

I don't image the doctor was very pleased with this last case, but you do see that Mr. McLean knew what he was about.

He certainly did a wonderful job all his life and, despite his death in 1969, his work will never be forgotten. Because there is no doubt that children will respond to a Teddy Bear far more readily than they will to the kindest of doctors. In some hospitals now there is a Teddy Bear with a rubber tube in his mouth for the purpose of administering anesthetics to children, the idea being to dispense with the frightening face mask used up till now.

Now some doctors even advise children undergoing operations to bring their bears with them, though I don't know how this fits in with hygienic precautions. But I do know that several hospitals in England keep a large selection of "Steiff" bears from which to choose; one of them buys at least fifty a year to replace faithful animals who have been pensioned off. In the children's ward of St. Luke's Hospital, Guilford, there is a giant Teddy called Boo-Boo who is five-foot-six and of course larger than any child in the ward.

But it is not only in physical mishaps that the Teddy Bear can have such beneficial effects; there are many examples of people living under severe mental tension being helped by them. It would seem that adults willingly turn to inanimate objects when the human element has let them down. Again and again there is concrete proof that a state of mind can be improved by the companionship of a Teddy; there is a steadying quality about a Teddy Bear which must influence the owner. Teddy's placid acceptance of everything and his serene composure, which has no smugness about it, can often bring a sense of proportion back and make you realize what the important things in life are and aren't. For a start, you can't imagine him running for a bus or a train, can you, or getting furious at the minor irritations and frustrations of modern living.

Helen Lovejoy certainly saw what it was all about. Confined

to bed in 1907 and short of funds, she suddenly had a brain wave, which I will let her describe in her own words:

> *To stare fixedly at a bedpost would not seem inspirational or help to solve a serious financial problem. Undoubtedly the stare would have remained wooden and meaningless as far as the post itself was concerned. The vitalizing influence was my little daughter's Teddy Bear. There he perched, one arm raised as if to arrest attention. There was something so optimistic in his attitude that it took hold of me and lifted me out of the Slough of Despond into which I had fallen. Like a flash it came to me what I would attempt: this absurd Teddy should earn money for me. I would have his photograph taken and send him out as a Valentine for the children. Could I interest a friend, an artist photographer, in the scheme? He might think the subject too trivial to merit his attention and time. But no! My enthusiasm and confidence were imparted to him. A fetching likeness was secured, halftones made and soon reproduced on cards. Teddy's picture, with his greeting underneath, was presented to the public.*

TO MY VALENTINE

One spot in my heart	*Keep a little bear spot.*
Is a little bear:	*In your heart for me;*
It need not be so, if	*You'll find me faithful*
You will live there.	*As Teddy B."*

> *Teddy was a winner from the start: phenomenally so. President Roosevelt was at the height of his popularity and that created favorable conditions for our Teddy. Not only the children but the grownups succumbed to his appeal. Orders came in faster than I could handle alone and assistants were engaged to help me deliver to the dealers. Later, other jingles were written for Teddy's use. A public bear, no less than a public lion, must prove versatile if he would*

retain prestige, and for several seasons Teddy held his own.

I wonder if any other Teddy Bear can boast of having contributed so materially to the support of a family!

In concluding the evidence on the efficacy of the bear's healing powers, I shall give you the details of two actual cases in which he saved lives beyond any shadow of a doubt.

Once when a German child fell from the fourth floor (American translation: fifth floor!) clutching her Teddy, she landed on top of it, breaking her fall, and suffered only minor injuries.

What happened to the bear is not disclosed. I wonder if he has been preserved in a glass case — like the animal who saved a baby's life in Hertfordshire, England. He intercepted a careless shot, fired probably by a poacher. The bullet just missed the occupant of a pram, who was cuddling his bear at the time. A grateful mother had Teddy embalmed for posterity.

But I'm *not* going to leave you in a cheerful mood at the end of this chapter. Did you know that Teddy Bears for children are included in all regular shipments to Vietnamese hospitals?

Teddies as Alter Ego's and Confidantes

Someone soft and warm
Someone quiet and understanding,
Always willing to listen,
Always willing to play,
Any time of the day,
Always there,
Teddy Bear.

In a poem by Judith Robins, the whole thing is put pretty accurately, for Teddy's constant availability as a listener is one of the qualities which has made him so outstanding and satisfying as a friend. I think all of us can remember the agony we went through in our early days trying to communicate with other human beings. Even then we could recognize the "Listening Face" so cruelly trying to convince us that we had its owner's undivided attention, while its owner was in fact either washing up, reading, writing, or thinking about a thousand other things. The result of this comparative neglect was that we had to pin our faith and reliance on someone else. And who better than a stolid, extremely interested, and undistractable Teddy?

Certainly one owner of a Cinnamon bear (a popular model at the beginning of the century) agrees with me: "I really do believe that he and I were closer than any human friends I ever had. Whatever my mood, he silently listened and sympathized with me. When I was ten I took a plane trip alone and the plane caught fire before we even took off. I was so scared but Cinnamon never flinched. I would have been terrified if it hadn't been for his strength and his hand to hold."

So many children look to this seemingly inanimate object as a protector. A young lady of fourteen is emphatic on this point: "My Teddy taught me to be loyal and to stand up for my convictions. He never forsook me. In turn, I sheltered him even in the face of the ridicule of brothers and sisters. He's someone I can love without thought of jealousy. He makes me easier to live with, as together we work out a solution to my problems. In short, he's something like God except that everyone has God and only I have my Teddy Bear."

The association of Teddy with the Almighty is not as rare as you might think. A small boy had been extremely naughty and had scratched his aunt's antique spinet. The aunt got pretty tetchy and told him that if he didn't stop, she would hurt something *he* loved. The boy stopped immediately and ran crying to his room, followed hot-foot by his mother. She was amazed to hear him saying to his Teddy Bear: "Poor Teddy, you're just like Jesus!" His mother asked him what he meant by that. "Well," sobbed Fred. "Just like Jesus, Teddy is going to have to suffer for my sins."

There is, of course, great danger in getting totally obsessed by any object, even a Teddy Bear. You can lose all sense of proportion. And with alarming results. A lady from Illinois told me of the tremendous part a Teddy played in her daughter's life. When the daughter got married, she announced to her husband: "My Teddy Bear sleeps with me, and if ever you hurt it, I'll divorce you." Not surprisingly, the couple had their problems. Finally the husband persuaded her to go to a psychiatrist. She was treated by him for six weeks, but they were getting nowhere until the subject of her Teddy was brought up. At this she jumped up and shouted: "You'll never get out of me what my Teddy Bear means to me!" and left, never to return. She, however, returned to her mother, who offered to wash the Teddy, which was dirty and torn, but the girl would not let her, "in case he got hurt." Her fear of this was so intense that she kept the bear in a small rocking chair and said over and over to him: "No one will ever hit you or hurt you." Teddy was a completely real person to her—so real that she was constantly asked if she could hear him breathing and talking! This, mind you, was a grown woman.

Loyal and trusted confidants

The reality of a Teddy Bear for a *child* is even more intense and cannot, in fact, be overmagnified. This is what sensitive parents do their best to understand. A clergyman from an Episcopal church in Pennsylvania told me about his worry when at the age of five he found that not only were his parents going to have another child, but they intended to call it Teddy. As he already had a Teddy, he informed them that it was out of the question because "we can't have two Teddies in the same house." So the incoming brother was called Robert and all was well in the household. "Teddy still lives," added the Reverend.

Sometimes a Teddy Bear can come overwhelmingly to represent nonexistent or inadequate parents. I know a very moving story of a small orphaned boy who had been buffeted around among various relatives. A homely couple without children thought of adopting him, and with this in view, invited him to spend the weekend with them. He arrived, in the dirtiest clothes, with an indescribably filthy Teddy Bear.

The lady of the house gave the little boy a bath and then set his friend aside while she went to get him clean clothes. After they had tucked the boy into bed they heard water running in the bath. When they peeped in to see what was going on, there he was — giving Teddy a severe scrubbing. He told them that he wanted to stay in their house, which meant that Teddy must be just as clean as he was or they might chuck them *both* out. He squeezed the bear gently to wring him out and hung him in the back yard to dry, but close to the window so that he could keep an eye on him. "You see," the boy explained, "he's been through so much with me."

Age has nothing to do with it. Adults who as children formed deep attachments to their animals have no intention of abandoning them until they are forced to, like the Florida lady who sent me Stevie because he was getting to be too much of a responsibility. But a lady in Connecticut has a friend who has hardly ever left her side since 1906. He has always been thought of as human by children and grandchildren and has never missed giving Christmas and birthday gifts.

Patched and repatched, he luckily has half a dozen knit suits with socks to match. "I only hope he will hold up as long as I do," says another Sinnamon's owner. "Then he is to be cremated with me. These arrangements have all been made with the undertaker, who has seen him."

The problem of what will happen to their bears after they themselves die obviously worries a lot of elderly owners, and a maiden lady of sixty-five has solved it by inserting a codicil in her will. Her three-foot Teddy, whom she still treats with the utmost respect, will share her coffin.

And it isn't only the elderly who are faced with decisions of this sort, alas. A Kentucky lady I heard from had a very sad tale to tell. Her five-year-old son died of leukemia holding a Teddy in his arms. The distraught mother took what she thought at the time was the only course possible:

> *I'm sure you'll be shocked to know that I had my son's small Teddy Bear put in his casket and buried with him. At the time of his death the thought of his being buried without at least one of his toys had been unbearable* [curious adjective to use and yet how appropriate], *so I chose his small bear. For a while I was pleased to know that boy and bear were together but I'll have to admit there are times when I regret it. It sounds crazy but I almost feel I buried the bear alive, certainly with its eyes open and still useful. So my wish for the second bear, which I bought to replace the original, is that he be immortal. I'm going to try and have him handed down from generation to generation. I've only just realized that I've never given the new bear a name, so I've christened him Robert Bull. For my son and you.*

It is impossible not to be moved by this, although few people will understand the depths (or heights) love of this kind will reach. Sometimes an ardent arctophilist will try desperately to free himself or herself from the involvement such an attachment brings in its wake. But

Miss Geldart and her three bears

he had better proceed somewhat warily, for the truth is that one never knows at what age one may need again the support of this childhood friend. It is certain, in any case, that the very old have almost as much reason for hanging on to him as adolescent children. A letter from an Illinois lady about her mother is illuminating. In the rest home, where the old lady (she is seventy-nine) lives, eight of the twelve inhabitants on the first floor have Teddy Bears with them "at all times." My correspondent ends with the observation: "These people must turn to their Teddy Bears in place of the children they have had."

To get off a slightly gloomy tack, let's consider the names which are given to the dear little fellows. In a British survey of statistics concerning three hundred and fifty bear-owning children, it was disclosed that forty-five percent of them called their friend Teddy because, as so many pointed out, "He IS a Teddy." Many of them had added in the questionnaire "OF COURSE," as though this were the only available name. Five percent favored diminutives of the word, and Tedkin, Big Ted, Little Ted, or plain Ted were much in evidence. One lady bear was named Tedwina because "he's a she not a him."

In the remaining groups there were a lot of obvious bear names. Sooty and Yogi (from British TV cartoons), Rupert from a strip ditto, Brumas and Panda (from the real thing at the zoo), and Pooh from You Know Where. Other popular choices were Honey, Honeybunch, Sugar, Candy, Treacle, Syrup, and Toffee " 'cos he looks so sweet."

Ordinary boys' names appeared rarely; when they did, the bear had usually been called after a favorite school friend, uncle, or even father. Descriptive names such as Cuddles, Tubby, Growly, Woolly, Ginger, or Curly—all bestowed for obvious reasons— were quite common.

Every one of the unusual names had been bestowed by an imaginative father. These included Polyphemus ("because he has only one eye"), Pythagoras ("because my sister hates geometry"), and Gladly ("this last because he's cross-eyed and we sing about him in a hymn 'Gladly My Cross I'd Bear'").

Almost two-eyed Cooper

Shad

One-Eyed Connolly

Hunny Bear

It's odd that "Theodore" is so comparatively rarely used, though I must say I have never had second thoughts about *my* bear's christening. But I do know that Teddies with unlikely names lead particularly adventurous lives. A lady from Michigan was devoted to her bear, Levi. Her preacher said at one time that if he could have his way he would destroy every Teddy. It was therefore singularly unfortunate that he should marry the young lady's aunt. A bow was put on Levi to celebrate the occasion and he was then safely hidden in a closet at his owner's house, where the wedding ceremony took place.

A bear called Tibby, who has crammed a great deal into his life, belonged to a Mrs. Kabell. She got him from Selfridge's in 1909. He lived in England until 1916, when he sailed for South Africa, through waters alive with U-boats, in the *Kenilworth Castle*. (On her return voyage the ship was torpedoed and sunk.)

In Africa he traveled with Mrs. Kabell's father, who was a film director of documentaries about native life and animals. Tibby was apparently looked on with awe by the residents and treated as if he were a "familiar" or "spirit." Later he went to Mauritius and dabbled in the Maiburg Lagoon, where mini-octopi darted about nibbling his feet. Later he sailed for Australia, encountering on the way a sea-spout (twister) and a hurricane. In New Zealand, only an earthquake hit him. Home to America via the South Sea Islands, Vancouver, San Francisco, New York, and Vermont, where he lived quietly and happily, until Mrs. Kabell's death in 1968. He has now joined Colonel Henderson's fine collection of Teddies where he lives a quiet life reminiscing with his chums.

My sister-in-law's sister, Joan Paton, had a very special bear, Bouncer by name. He came off a Christmas tree in 1906 and is still alive and kicking. He never left her side till she was fifteen, "except for my confirmation," Mrs. Paton tells me. He was an ardent theatre-goer and saw everything she went to. He sat on her shoulder so as to have an uninterrupted view of the stage. (There is no record of a customer sitting behind saying, "Will you kindly remove your bear, madam?")

He was given his name after one of the characters in a book called *Two Little Bears*. Gabrielle, my sister-in-law, was presented with a white bear, whom she called Gretchen after the other bear. In 1914 it was rechristened Blanchette because, owing to the outbreak of war, her previous name was deemed unpatriotic.

For her tenth birthday Bouncer's owner was given a cake with small Teddy Bears on it instead of candles. Mrs. Paton remembers their names to this day. The boy bears were Bertram, Bernard, Brian, Boniface, and Bruce, while the girls were called Belinda, Barbara, Beryl, Berenice, and Beatrice. Bouncer had an extensive wardrobe and his owner recalls her extreme pleasure when Father Christmas presented him with a mackintosh and galoshes so that he need no longer be carried inside her coat if it rained on their daily outings.

"My whole childhood was bounded by Bouncer and I remember so well the awful moment at Hunstanton when I thought he was going to jump out of my arms and drop through a crack in the pier."

But the Moment of Truth arrived when Mrs. Paton caught scarlet fever at the age of fifteen. Bouncer remained with her until it was discovered what the illness actually was. "So the poor thing had to be baked in the oven after being disinfected and I think it was then when he ceased to be such an inseparable companion. Perhaps I realized that he really could NOT be alive. I was always positive that he was a real live person. But when he survived the baking and looked the same I must have realized the truth. After all I was *fifteen*."

So much for Bouncer and disillusion. On the other hand, Shadrack McDermid is more real to his owner after twenty-seven years than he was when they first met. She is a P.R.O., who used to work for an airline in Florida. Theodore and I had a delightful time with them both in New York and I was deeply impressed by Shad's activities. He seems to have spent his life keeping people happy and has pen pals all over the world. It all started after an article about him had appeared in a newspaper. Since then he has gathered a family around him, which numbers more than a hundred. The Shad Pad is run on disciplined

80

lines, and if the master is called away, Ignatz, a big but blind bear once left on his doorstep, steps in to assume command.

Shad has a voluminous correspondence and deals mainly with people's emotional and career problems. He is a sort of Universal Uncle. He has dispatched relatives to keep the company of lonely soldiers in the Far East, comforted the unhappy and maladjusted, and been lent to close friends who might need temporary companionship.

"Shad has had a long and useful life, cheering and comforting people," says Miss Betty McDermid. "In short, he exists for one thing—to make life more bearable."

Did you know, by the way, there was a Teddy Bear Club? It has no subscription, no committee, no meeting place, and no funds. "But it exists universally in the subconscious mind. All those who have an affection for Teddy Bears may belong. In this way new friends are made and the common bond of Teddy Bear consciousness binds together whole groups of people of otherwise diverse intersts."

This is what the president of The Teddy Bear Club believes, anyhow. He is Robert Henderson, until recently a colonel in a well-known Scottish regiment, and he has supplied me with riveting bits of information and spurred me on by his enthusiasm for his subject. Possessor of just one hundred and thirty bears himself, he knows every nook and cranny of beardom.

Colonel Henderson corresponds with an unlimited number of people and it was one of these who nominated him unofficially as president of the T.B.C. He takes this appointment very seriously. All the news of the Teddy Bear world seems to filter through to him and he has told me of many factual cases in which the animal's power to help has been proved. A Teddy who was consoling a sad young girl whose engagement had been broken off; one that had taken the place of a beloved cat an elderly lady had lost; one who was helping a girl return to good health after a nervous breakdown; and yet another who was comforting a widower.

All these Teddy Bears were functioning as focal points for affec-

Mrs. Gillian Robinson and her family (bottom), *Colonel Henderson and his army of bears* (top)

Cathy and the Murphy bears

tion in the lives of lonely and distressed persons. One hard-working housekeeper has found that talking to a bear lessens the drudgery of her task. Many are the roles that the Teddy Bear can play in the lives of people in all walks of life. The colonel goes on to give a superb generalization of the whole mystique of Edward Bear: "He permeates the whole structure of society. This is because he is a truly international figure who is nonreligious and yet universally recognized as a symbol of love. He represents friendship, and so is a powerful instrument of good will, a wonderful ambassador of peace, functioning as a leavening influence amid the trials and tribulations of life in the modern world."

Leavening influence. I know exactly what he means. Just to look at a Teddy when one is upset is a help. It may sound silly but that slightly absurd face brings things back into focus almost at once, as not only Colonel Henderson knows.

His own collection must be unique in the world for its variety; besides lots of the popular cuddly ones of all shapes, sizes, and makes, his Teddies are in the shape of money boxes, teapots, cruet sets, candles, paperweights, chessmen, bottles, cake and table ornaments, matchboxes, souvenirs, brooches, pendants, castings, carvings, fretwork, shoes, tobacco jars, umbrella stands, puppets, and ashtrays.

They are constructed out of plastic, wax, soap, papier-mâché, cardboard, wood, china, earthenware, glass, fur, paper, sugar, chocolate, soapstone, bone, ivory, gold, silver, bronze, brass, lead, metal, and pipe-cleaner material.

The colonel is especially proud of his 1903 Teddy—a "Mark One model" he calls him. This animal, who is two years older than his owner, started life as the property of the colonel's elder brother, and then was shared by the two boys. Later he was inherited by the colonel's daughter, Cynthia, and changed his sex—well, the girl insisted on dressing him in a frilly skirt, so he *had* to become a Teddy Girl!

During the war Colonel Henderson carried as a mascot a miniature bear. Throughout the Northwest European campaign they served together on General Montgomery's staff.

His smallest Teddy is thirty millimeters tall and the smallest bear model (of silver) is 0.3 inches (seven millimeters), which he thinks must be the smallest bear in the world. But I have two rivals, both of whom are enchanting. One is a minute brown creature crocheted by a dear friend's grandmother about fifty years ago. The other, a tiny gold bear from Tiffany's, with movable arms and legs, is for wearing on a chain round the neck. This was sent anonymously to me one day in New York and I would like to take this opportunity of thanking the donor for the delightful thought.

Recently Colonel Henderson had a letter from a lady asking if she could have one of the small bears from his collection. He sent her one, and got a letter of thanks. The lady explained that she had been very lonely, but found that if she carried a little Teddy Bear in her handbag, she had only to produce it and someone would start a conversation.

"You see," she wrote, "I am blind."

Teddy in the Adult World

I love my little Teddy Bear
He's such a friendly fellow,
His fur, beautiful and soft,
Is neither brown nor yellow.
He plays but never quarrels with me,
And keeps me gay and jolly,
And I don't have to punish him
As often as my Dolly.
He's such a quiet little chap,
No impish schemes he hatches,
He never barks, he has no fleas,
At least he never scratches.

So wrote Mrs. Eulia Smith-Zimman, who always longed for a Teddy Bear but whose parents believed in more practical toys. She wrote this verse after she was married, when an older sister presented her with her first Teddy Bear.

I do hope Mr. Smith-Zimman was sympathetic to the whole thing and didn't leave her on the spot, but we adult arctophilists have to face a good deal of derision and disbelief. Sometimes when I'm describing some of Theodore's foibles or quirks I see a look of terror come into the eyes of the listener. For it is usually incomprehensible to the person who has never possessed or even wanted a Teddy Bear that an adult can be so passionately attached to what is apparently only a stuffed toy. But then I feel the same sort of thing when people start going on about their cars, yachts, houses, or bank balances, all of which seem to me far more inanimate than Teddy.

I am no longer even remotely self-conscious when I talk about him. Not so very long ago I carried a large metal Teddy Bear in my arms back from America to England. He had been specially made for me by two brilliant young metal sculptors called Al and Jack who run a firm called Griffin Design. He has gold amber eyes and a sort of gold crocheted body. He was (and indeed is) completely transparent and absolutely beautiful. I had a few qualms when I approached the Customs officials, as Teddies are regarded with the gravest suspicion in these quarters. And quite rightly so, for just the other day a large Teddy was found lying on a bench at Rio de Janeiro airport, containing five hundred and twelve pairs of nylon panties and two hundred and ten dresses. It appears that their bodies are frequently used for smuggling dope and jewels as well.

So I was expecting a little trouble at London Airport, but apart from an occasional raised eyebrow, Teddy was passed through the Customs without reaction. He had attracted quite a lot of attention on the plane, of course. I suppose a few years ago I wouldn't have dared behave in this way. In those days I was totally unconscious of the vast underground Teddy Bear movement which exists in the adult world. It still astonishes me how many intelligent people have got seriously caught up in it. I got several letters referring to the effect a recent television appearance had had on the little animals: "As I listened," one viewer wrote in, "Teddy (aged sixty) sat in a chair and took in every word. At the time I was busy unpacking a coat with which I hope to recover him."

Another viewer also had wardrobe problems: "Shortly before the program came on, we had been discussing how we could wash Teddy Nude's (yes, that's his name) yellow tummy. I said I couldn't bear to wash him, let alone hang him on the line to dry afterwards. How extraordinary that you should mention this problem yourself only a few minutes afterwards."

Neither of these correspondents would have agreed with the Czech poet Rilke, who was full of resentment against dolls and Teddy Bears because "they refuse to absorb any of the tenderness lavished on them." He also made the intolerable (to say nothing of intolerant) affirmation that "affection spent on them is wasted. They teach the uselessness of love; they destroy love by destroying all belief in it."

Fiddle-de-de, Mr. Rilke! He had obviously been thwarted in love before he wrote that farrago of nonsense. He doesn't even realize that no love can be entirely wasted, even love that is not reciprocated. The mere fact that a Teddy Bear or, at worst, a doll has been chosen to confide in is a testimony to their usefulness. The *feeling* that loyalty and love are returned is what is important for the child growing up.

And for adults, too. Did you know that an English insurance broker, called Henry Middleditch, sued his former wife for the return of an "eighteenth-century table, a cut-glass decanter, and his Teddy Bear"?

A lady called Mrs. James Dow McCallum commented interestingly on this in the *Hanover Gazette* of November 5, 1964:

> Mr. Middleditch has my complete sympathy and I hope an understanding judge gave him immediate custody of the bear, which probably didn't mean a thing to his wife. But why do you suppose he left it behind in the first place? When I finally put away childish things in favour of a husband and family, I brought my Teddy Bear with me. I wept into his golden fur, pillowed my head on his comfortable stomach and did my homework under his benevolent eye. He was my private house-god, my personal Lar. On that happy occasion when my dearest friend and I worked out a precautionary fire drill for our bears, Brownie was not included in the string of animals we lowered from the fifth-floor window, since there was never any question but that Brownie would be with me, whatever my fate, should the apartment go up in flames. This was fortunate, as we had underestimated the accumulated weight of our animals, with the result that a shower of Teddy Bears fell on Broadway to the surprise and indignation of some innocent passers-by. I do hope the London chap got his bear

Teddy in action

back. It makes such a charming picture; the eighteenth-century table, and decanter appropriately filled, and for company Mr. Edward Bear.

Teddies are no strangers to the law courts. I even know one (though not intimately) who was produced as evidence of adultery. And recently in a trial at the Old Bailey in London, Sugar, a small blue nylon Teddy, sat with a card around his neck labeled "Exhibit No. 56." He was partly responsible for jailing two men for receiving stolen cars. After the trial was over, he was brought back to Amanda, his owner, by the detective sergeant in charge of the case.

On the other hand, a police constable in England was cleared of stealing a bear. His defending counsel advanced the plea, a little naïvely *I* think: "Is a man of his age, getting toward the end of his service in the force, likely to take away a Teddy Bear intending to keep it?"

The only person I know who actually stole a Teddy is the actor Paul Scofield, who admitted his crime to me some forty years later. He had always wanted one; he saw a bear lying around, which he annexed; no one seemed to mind at the time, but he had to return it later.

As for people I *don't* know who stole Teddies, on November 16, 1966, somebody or bodies stole six hundred pounds' worth of them (before the pound was devalued). There were three hundred of them—two feet high, with noses of black plastic and bells in their ears—sitting, minding their own business in a warehouse in the East End of London, and then they were gone.

Contrariwise, Douglas Gordon Goody, jailed for his part in the Great Train Robbery, has been making Teddy Bears in one of Her Majesty's prison workshops. And more power to him!

On a slightly classier scale, Mr. Donald Peatling Scott, heir to an industrial fortune, sued the French actress Corinne Calvet for the return of a cane sword, which once belonged to Errol Flynn, and a painting of a Teddy Bear. She'd painted a still life of carnations, a picture of two rabbits, and one of a Teddy Bear. She said he could have the rabbit one as long as she got the other two.

Well, *that's* something. Teddies do have a knack, too, of taking a hand in affairs of the heart. I remember the beautiful Samantha Eggar's bringing her large Teddy Bear to her wedding to Tom Stern in Chelsea, London. Teddy naturally sat in the front pew on the "bride's side." Said Samantha as she drove up to the church with him: "He's been present at all the most important moments of my life so far."

I was present at that wedding but not, unfortunately, at any of those celebrated by a lady from North Attleboro, who tells me that the constant solace of her very miserable childhood was a big Teddy Bear with orange-reddish hair on it. "A series of unhappy marriages convinced me that I was unconsciously looking for my Teddy Bear and I eventually found a man who greatly resembles one."

You'd be *astonished* at how many ladies have confessed that they have married bearlike gents. I find it highly dubious that it ever happens the other way round. I mean, I can imagine a man marrying a girl because she was "cuddly" but not because she looked like a Teddy Bear! (There are, you know, cases of the female of the species; I even had a letter from a "Teddy Bearess" who lived, of all places, in Barcelona.)

And in order to make this survey complete in every way, whatever the cost to readers' feelings, here is the moment to tell you that three gentlemen have admitted to having their first sexual experience with a Teddy Bear.

Some unmarried ladies go so far as to say: "Anybody who takes me must take my bears or stay out of my life." I am thinking particularly of an English lady who quite obviously meant it. She is nearly forty and her whole life seems bear-beset. Her bears' costumes vary from frilled gingham to lace-edged print and silk taffeta. Some wear tiny bracelets and others pendants at the neck. Goodness! However, though a few years ago this sort of costuming would have been deemed a whit "sissy," it can now be said that Miss Lockheart's bears are very much with it. She certainly looks after them devotedly enough in her bed-sitting-room (they must surely take up most of it!), but then she says that they are "an integral part" of her existence. At night she "borrows" her own bed back from them and pops them into a large trunk purchased for this special purpose.

This habit of littering the room with Teddy Bears must dismay skeptical callers. I know some otherwise normal chartered accountants called Tree and Son who have seven bears, all of whom sit either on the settee or chairs. As they are called Kerry Mac, Parker Hill, Kapeno, Upsi Duck, What-a-Myth, Edward Mode, and Spook, it must make for quite a good party when things get really swinging chez Tree. The bears are apparently called after horses or dogs on whom the owners have won substantial sums. And though they are mainly kept at home, one, I am assured, takes pride of place at the board-room table.

A couple in Washington seem to me to go about as far as you *can* go with this sort of thing. They have a small bear, ten inches high, whom they take everywhere, put to bed at night, and rouse in the morning. His jackets, sweaters, and ties are all made for him. He has his own chair and his own bank account (accumulated from his weekly allowance and winnings on the scores of sporting events). Not unnaturally, he is a benevolent despot.

"Neither my husband nor I would be surprised to come home in the evening and see him walking about our apartment," states the distaff side of his owners.

"Our bear is like a spoiled child. He must have his way or his say. We leave lights and the TV on for him in the evening. Some of our friends think we are a little peculiar."

I wonder what their friends would have thought of the Dalys of Essex, England, and their large family of bears. "Our chaps rather like to feel that they are among the best-dressed bears in the country. They have at least two summer and two winter suits each (plus caps and boots) and our number 3 bear" [they have twenty-three] "who is

93

Danger: Bears at work

rather naval, has been heard to talk about going into 'blues' or 'whites.' " The wardrobe is supplied by Mrs. Daly's mother. The bears are all named and numbered and have come from all over the world. Lapsang Soochong came from China, Carlo Bergonzi from Italy, Franz Joseph from Austria, Pendennis Arwanack from Cornwall, and Boris Gregory from Poland. The latter is also known in certain circles as 007. Number 10 (Cockney George) was picked out of the gutter in the East End of London. It was around Christmas, so Mrs. Daly felt sure he must have been intended as a present and turned him into the police, who sent a squad car to fetch him. But after a month he returned, having found no claimant.

Other distinguished members of the Daly family include Rupert from the Channel Islands, who is extremely musical and attends all the concerts which the Dalys patronize. He is addicted particularly to Mozart and claims to be the only Teddy Bear actually to have sat on the composer's piano in Salzburg.

Then there is Bruno, who is Swiss and therefore money-conscious. He is in charge of the piggy bank, and when the Dalys eat out abroad, always sits at table to make sure that they are not being overcharged.

Ned, one of the British bears, is a cricket fan and has in his day attracted quite a bit of attention watching his home team (Somerset) play.

All the Daly bears have very strong personalities and fulfill their various functions properly and unfailingly.

The wife of a Scots judge has a collection of thirteen bears, all dressed in naval uniform, from ratings to one full admiral. My young informant, a relative of the lady, was fairly surprised to see them ranged in line on her drawing-room sofa and flabbergasted a few days later when she went to see her off on a long journey by train. For there, in the railway carriage, were all the bears, taking up a whole side. "I cannot remember anyone offering any comment, so I suppose I took it as one of the inexplicable things which grownups did."

It isn't reported whether the little passengers were charged their fare. A lady on a London bus had to pay for the Teddies who accompanied her. Their tummies were apparently rumbling so much that an insensitive conductor made her fork up (half price). I think they must have both been "Growlers," a type of bear which was at that time very popular.

There is no doubt that Teddies enjoy traveling very much. I've run across many actual emigrants who seem to have very nicely survived transplantation. Some, like Petrovic (called after Peter the Great, naturally), come from places as far away as Yugoslavia. His owner, Miss Zita Zore, once had twenty-five bears in Belgrade and now has only Petrovic, who is keen on vodka and lives on East 86th Street in New York City.

The extent of the Teddy Bear's aptitude for travel is not known, so I don't know *what* will happen to a lemondrop-eating lady from Virginia who is convinced that she was reincarnated from a Teddy Bear —and that she will return to being one when she leaves "this people world." She has therefore instructed her husband to be kind to all lemondrop-eating bears after she's gone.

I am assured by a lady who works for the British Navy that many of the officers and men take Teddies to sea with them and that these Teddies are known as "pocket diplomats." I doubt it's the same with the American Navy, where we're up against the old "virility status" hang-up. (I can hear Theodore snorting over my shoulder and repeating "virility status" in a tone of disgust.)

A gentleman who owes a big debt to his Teddy Bear is Mr. David White of London. He was asked to a party a while ago and met a young lady called Claire Emmett. (He had been invited by mistake for another D. White.) Some time later Miss Emmett gave him a Teddy Bear. This prompted Mr. White to ask him if he should marry her. The bear said yes he should and he did and I should jolly well hope they are all living happily ever after and raising a small family of Teddy Bears.

It is *essential* for an arctophilist to find a marriage partner who, if not one himself, at least understands the position. A young lady recently got a lovely surprise at her wedding when her much-loved Teddy turned up at the reception in a special suit made by her mother. Her husband, in responding to the toast, mentioned Teddy as part of the family, as was only right and proper.

As Colonel Henderson says: "Teddy Bear consciousness binds together whole groups of people," not to mention couples.

And from couples to threesomes. In an anonymous letter to me, the writer tells of an astonishing experience in which a Teddy Bear apparently changed her life. Or rather *three* did!

> *I am an only child and my mummy died when I was little and my daddy is away a lot on business, but I have a Teddy Bear which I love a lot. But my wicked stepmother did not like this and one day she took my Teddy Bear and went away with it into the forest (did you know that there were forests in New Mexico?) and she hid it there and came back and said to me I have hid your Teddy Bear in the forest and it will die, how do you like them apples, kid?*
>
> *I ran into the forest to look for my Teddy. I come across this cute little house, so I went up to it to ask for a Coke. But was nobody home and no Coke in the icebox but there on the table was bowls of yummy Wheateana and I was so hungry that I eat one of them. Then I went upstairs for a zizz, what with all that walking and Wheateana and all, so I just lay down on one of the beds and went off.*
>
> *Well, to cut a long story short, who should this cute little shack belong to but three bears! The real thing yet! And they come back while I'm in the sweet and dreamless and wake me up and threaten to call the cops. But as I point out to them, what kind of a case do they have on me over one lousy bowl of Wheateana and pretty lumpy at that?*
>
> *So then we get to talking about bears and what not*

and I tell them how much I love my Teddy, and by this time we are all laying around the beds and one of the bears says did you ever think of trying the real thing, honey, and I says no, and one thing leads to about eight others and somehow I ain't left yet. I want you to know that they are swinging bears.

If you use my story, withhold my name or my lumpy stepmother may get to find me and try to horn in on my act. Perhaps you could just call it the Story of G* and this would be our secret.

Now, to bring you sharply back to reality, what about the middle-aged gent who queued all night outside a big store to buy a monster Teddy in a sale? He said it was for his daughter, but the assistant wasn't so sure.

*Goldilocks

Let Us Now Praise Famous Bears

I'm really Edward George St. Clare,
Aubrey Adolphus de la Bear
Son and heir of the Baron Bear,
But you may call me Teddy Bear.
*So please me, squeeze me, I don't care.**

It is about time we stopped considering people and their attitudes toward Teddies and started dealing with the Bear Roll of Honor. We have so many famous and distinguished bears of whom to be proud, but I think it only right and proper to lead off with the One Who Climbed the Matterhorn. You heard! *You* haven't got cloth ears! The Matterhorn. My authority is no less unimpeachable than the curator of the Alpine Museum, Zermatt—Mr. Karl Lehner. He sent me the information in French.

An Italian Alpine climber called Walter Bonnati conquered the north slopes of the mountain on February 22, 1965. It took him the better part of five days, but he doubts if he could have done it at all without the help of a small Teddy he carried in his rucksack. Small, yellow, and very adventurous, he belonged to the children of the local hotel Alpenblick.

The first three nights were bearable, but on the fourth Mr. Bonnati was in despair. There was a terrible wind and the cold was terrible, too. His morale was at zero; and snow fell from the sky, freezing on him as he tried to sleep. He was so miserable he thought of cutting the rope and ending it all in a few seconds.

Suddenly he remembered the Teddy Bear and took him out of

*From an autograph album dated February 6, 1912.

101

his comparatively warm hiding place. He spent the night talking to him about everything under the stars, and even got as far as confessing his "sins" ("péchés" in Mr. L's French), to all of which the Teddy listened with rapt attention. Indeed, when the first light of dawn came, he was still listening to the climber's life story.

Mr. Bonnati pressed on to the top of the mountain in victory. On his return, he told the bear's owners that their little friend had saved his life. So if any of you are thinking of attempting the Matterhorn, I would advise you to get in touch with the Pannatier children. Their Teddy Bear Zissi will direct you to the summit!

Another bear to be proud of is Mr. Woppit, who belonged to the late Donald Campbell, C.B.E. He was without doubt the fastest Teddy in the world. The two first met in 1957 when Campbell's manager, Peter Barker, placed the animal in the cockpit of the jet-propelled Bluebird hydroplane before Campbell made his attempt at the world's water speed record. Mr. Woppit has three records to his credit, as a matter of fact, for he achieved 260-3 miles an hour at Coniston Water in May 1959. He was also with Campbell when they both survived the fastest automobile crash in history on the Bonneville Salt Flats in Utah in 1960. They were traveling in the Proteus Bluebird and Campbell, lying in the hospital with a fractured skull, described the horror he felt when he realized that Mr. Woppit was still in the cockpit. An urgent radio message was dispatched and the bear was given a police escort to the hospital—only to discover after X-rays that he had his nose a bit out of joint but was otherwise none the worse for his adventure.

He is eight inches high and looks like a cross between a Koala and a baby bear. He is made of light brown fur fabric and wears green shoes and a rather tight scarlet jacket. His ears are green-lined too! He is named after a character which appeared in the first number of a popular children's comic called "Robin."

Mr. Woppit has now traveled at 403 m.p.h. on land. To have been the fastest on land *and* sea has so far been a distinction held only by Sir Malcolm and Donald Campbell and Mr. Woppit. Unfortunately, the latter is the sole survivor. He was found floating face downward after the tragedy which killed his friend in 1967. He is now cherished by Donald Campbell's widow, Tonia Bern, the cabaret star.

Another Teddy, cast in the heroic mold, who has had greatness thrust on him, is Rupert, who belongs to Janet, the daughter of George Villiers, the BBC's cookery expert. When the family was escaping from Nazi-occupied Norway during World War II, Rupert was about the only thing they were able to salvage in their haste. Adrift in the North Sea, they were making for the Shetland Islands when a British reconnaissance plane flew low over them. Janet was instructed to make Rupert wave at it. This she did. Later they were told that it was he, Rupert, who convinced the crew of the plane that the refugees must be British. I only hope Rupert was not a Steiff bear—because if he was, he must have felt a bit traitorous.

Then there was Old Brown Teddy. "He went to Burma in 1937 and escaped with Mummy in 1942. They had lots of adventures and Mummy always carried him even when the Japs bombed them." I culled this information from Miss Jennie Wade, aged six and a half, who called in person with her own bear Herbert. "Once I lost him in the country under a tree and my Gran sent me another called Honey. Then we found Herbert again and now I have two twins called Patty and Daisy and you can see them all if you like."

Sometimes the bear himself is a refugee on his own, as in the case of Edward Bear, who was born behind the iron curtain. At an early age (judging by state and color of fur, lines on paws, etc.) he made up his mind to leave. He crossed into Switzerland and got himself hidden in a bedside cupboard in a clinic frequented by foreigners. There, Mr. Carr, a high-ranking British civil servant, found him and felt empowered to offer him political asylum. Mrs. Carr celebrated the arrival of the defector into her household by hastily knitting a jacket for him. Her husband lent him an old tie, which he has never returned, as a matter of fact. He has been everywhere with the Carrs, and even crossed the Atlantic with them in the SS *United States*, where he was called "a cute little bear," an expression he took almost as much exception to as being described as "une fetiche" on the SS *France* on his return trip.

Mrs. Carr writes: "It's difficult not to sound whimsical about Teddy Bears. I can only say that some people feel they have a spirit. So you must forgive me if I feel Edward is quite real."

Teddies have never flinched from danger. It was no surprise to me to learn that there are several Teddies who have made parachute descents. The one attached to the Royal Military Academy at Sandhurst in England has made over three hundred. He has his own uniform, similar to that of an officer cadet. He also possesses his own parachute and has been frequently decorated.

One of the many soldiers who took their bears to the wars was an ex-Polish officer from the 1st Polish Armored Division. This Teddy was accorded the honorary rank of Bombardier and now, after spending many holidays there, is a "Junior Knight of Malta."

And now—ho-hum—to general bear name-dropping. The King of Thailand has traveled the world in state with his Teddy Bear. The late Prince Tulo of Siam (it must run in the family) had a minute one which he carried everywhere with him: the bear went to bed in a matchbox and didn't, apparently, miss a trick.

Prince Charles of England had a Teddy who accompanied him to school. When the Prince was four years old, there was a party given for him at Buckingham Palace and the band of the Grenadier Guards played his favorite tune—"The Teddy Bear's Picnic," naturally. The gathering itself was described as the most light-hearted in the White and Gold Room since Queen Victoria still had children "young enough to romp in the same spirit."

Several Teddies claim to have met their creator in person. And I'm not being blasphemous. The most likely candidate belonged to Mr. Walter Pelham, who was at Trinity College when President Theodore Roosevelt visited Cambridge University in 1905. Mr. Pelham's daughter tells me that her father and another Trinity chap lowered the animal by means of a string to face Mr. Roosevelt as he entered the quadrangle. One press report has it that the President actually stopped and shook hands with it. "The bear hung on my father's study wall ever after," wrote the lady, "and was something to look at when being chastised, or lectured, or when asking for money or telling lies about where one had been."

Both Theodore and I would have been thrilled had we met Mr. Roosevelt, but Miss Wynne Fairchild, of Minnesota, and her sister are very blasé about the whole thing. The President was visiting Omaha, where they lived at the time. "Mother took us down to the depot to shake his hand. She told us to be sure and bring our Teddy Bears, which we considered pretty ridiculous."

We all know about more recent Presidents' interest in the bear mystique. A Teddy sits proudly on the window sill of the John F. Kennedy childhood home nursery on Beals Street in Brookline, Massachusetts. And in one room of former President Johnson's ranch there is his crib and on it sits *his* Teddy Bear.

Apart from that snippet about Prince Charles, information about the British Royal Family and their involvement in the Teddy world is pretty scarce. The nearest I've been able to get is the mother of the Garter King at Arms (by appointment to H.M. the Queen), Sir Anthony Wagner, who possesses a valued Teddy much decorated in the war. Mrs. Wagner, his mother, told me that "Teddy would be glad if you would call and see him—by appointment"! That seems about as grand as you can get. She added: "I will ask the Queen's under-nurse, who was nurse to my son's children, if there are any notable bears at the Palace." Since no further dispatch has reached me so far, I fear that regal inter-nursery communication must have broken down.

By a curious coincidence, Garter King at Arms' cousin, Miss Rosemary Weir, wrote to tell me about his bear and how she abducted him when she was eight and on holiday in the country. "I took him to stay with a mutual (or should it be "common"?) aunt." This drove the future King at Arms predictably into a fury and the bear was restored forthwith.

Miss Weir must have been a very acquisitive young lady in those days, because she informs me that she possessed a Teddy senior to her cousin's. "If Garter K at A tries to make out that his bear is older than mine, have none of it. When Teddy joined me in 1907, Cousin Anthony was in no fit state to own anything, being as yet unborn."

Her own bear always wore wool next to the skin "and still does. And my cousin's sits on a special chair in his dressing room."

Many bears (and their friends) have written in to say that they are the Oldest Teddy Bear in the world. But excepting the original Presidential one, I am inclined to think that Colonel Henderson may very easily house the winner. Another hot contender is Sir Edward Bear, Bt., who belongs to Elizabeth Rimer of Ilford, England. He was bought in Switzerland by Elizabeth's great-grandfather and is sixty-six years old. He's had a bit of renovating since 1904 — several new noses and a smart set of brown suede paws. Also, he has lost his voice. But his eyes are still his own. And he has his hump. Manufacturers stopped putting humps on Teddies around 1906, so if you run across a behumped bear you may be sure he's over sixty. So pay him a bit of respect, won't you?

That was the period when there were bears on wheels, and a good many of them at that. Some had cords attached to their shoulders, which made them growl when they were pulled — and why not? Wouldn't you, under similar circumstances? The "Growler" for some time was all the rage. I heard an amusing story of one who was sent through the post. The parcel was delivered by a policeman who had instructions to watch it opened because the sender was suspected of contravening the law by sending a live animal through the post. The happy recipient still remembers the blood-curdling growls heard every time the parcel was tilted.

But to return to famous bears or, now, their famous owners. These include Dame Margot Fonteyn and her husband, who, I understand, was greatly comforted by one during his long illness, Nadia Nerina, Elvis Presley, the late Dorothy Gish, and Rose O'Neill, the originator of the Kewpie Doll.

And so to Winnie-the-Pooh! Ah, you'd been wondering when I was going to get around to that one, hadn't you? He has been with us so long that we almost take him for granted, and yet, in spite of his forty years, he seems more modern and "with it" than ever. In fact, his international reputation stands at an all-time high. In Britain a new Pooh cult has appeared. In the *Daily Mail* recently, Desmond Zwar affirmed that "the undergraduates of Britain have found a new hero. Students are gathering in rooms to dig spoons into pots marked 'Hunny' and to listen to readings on the best way to trap the 'heffalump.'"

At Oxford, smug Pooh addicts read about their hero from a Latin translation. At Hull University the eighty-strong Pooh Society has challenged all comers to a British Students Poohsticks and Hum Championship. (Poohsticks, for the uninitiated, are played by tossing sticks down from one side of the bridge and running to the other side to see whose floats through first; a "hum" is a Winnie-the-Pooh-written poem.)

At the new University of Essex, a hundred of the four hundred students gather regularly under the oak trees and listen to readers, holding red and green balloons, recount the Pooh adventures.

> 3 Cheers for Pooh!
> (For Who?)
> For Pooh –
> (Why, what did he do?)
> I thought you knew;
> He saved his friend from a wetting!

In Australia it's the same. Sydney University's Tiddlywinks Society even organized a Pooh Festival. A crowd of two hundred attended the opening but this soon swelled to five hundred for the major Pooh reading. And fifty braved terrible weather for a touching lamplight farewell to Pooh on the front lawn. He then left for the University of New South Wales, where equally enthusiastic demonstrations took place.

David Frankel, the Tiddlywinks Society's president, has sent me the program of the Pooh Festival, which lasted four days. Special attractions included a "Hummalong" and a "Heffalump Hunt"; "Hunny" and "Hunny and Haycorn Crackle" were readily available. And there were "Hum Sessions" and "Pooh Readings."

"The Farewell," Mr. Frankel reports, "was read by lantern light to the slow tolling of a cowbell and ended with a pathetic little procession of students trailing across the lawn behind the mournful skirl of a solitary bagpipe. Very moving. But a final Hum-tiddly-pom revived our spirits and we went away 'tiddly-pom-happy.'"

Mr. Frankel, who is a bit of a wit, as you can see, informs me that there is a Pooh Society in New Zealand, where they tend to play Pooh-sticks with live people.

There are many Pooh Societies all over America, too, and in universities especially the mystique thrives. It doesn't surprise me that Winnie-the-Pooh has become the darling of the Young Intelligentsia, particularly when I remember what an effect he had on the doyens of the Algonquin Round Table coterie in New York. This group, headed by Alexander Woollcott, included George Kaufman, Robert Benchley, Dorothy Parker, and other great and influential wits of the time, all of whom greeted the publication of the Milne works with rapture.

When We Were Very Young was the first to come out in the United States, in 1924. *Winnie-the-Pooh* arrived there in 1926, and thirty-six years later, in the spring of 1962, was still being reported to the *New York Times Book Review* as one of the top best-selling childrens' books. And yet E. P. Dutton, who publishes all the Milne work in America, tells me that their appeal was always general and that they have never looked on them as being principally for the juvenile reader. It is a fact that 9,644,000 hardbacks have been sold since 1926.

And what of Christopher Robin himself? He now runs a small bookshop in the West Country of England and has tried as far as possible to dissociate himself from any of the Poohaha which followed the publication of his father's books, to the success of which he has contributed so immeasurably. He wasn't even present at the party in 1966

Elderly Sir Ted knows what it feels like to be cuddled

REDBRIDGE'S newest knight sat back in his armchair, gave a supercilious grin and appeared to listen attentively while his owners told me of his 64 years devoted service.

Sir Edward Bear, Bart., now lives in Mapleleafe-gardens, Barkingside, the proud property of ten-year-old **Elizabeth Rimer.**

In case you hadn't guessed, Sir Edward is a Teddy bear — believed to be the world's oldest.

He began his life in 1904, in Berne, Switzerland, when Elizabeth's great - grandfather presented him to his four-year-old daughter.

Sir Edward — or Teddy as he was known to his friends in those days — was played with and passed on to Elizabeth's mother, **Mrs. Eileen Rimer.**

☆

It was at Christmas that he was knighted by the curator of the Victoria and Albert Museum.

The Rimer family had gone to see an exhibition of Victorian toys and Christmas cards when they spotted a bear in a glass case, made in 1908, claimed to be the world's oldest.

As bears were first made in 1903, the chances are that Sir Edward is the oldest — but Elizabeth is not parting with him. She agrees with her mother, who says:

"I couldn't bear to see him in a glass case. Bears are made to play with — and in any case, he's one of the family."

Sir Edward's 1968 renovations include a new nose and two suede paws, but he still sports his original eyes — and no glasses!

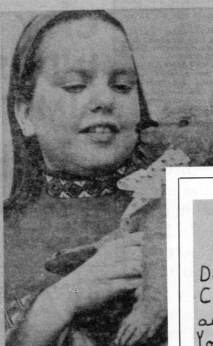

● Elizabeth . . . give

---

19 MAPLELEAFE GDNS.
BARKINGSIDE
ILFORD ESSEX.

Dear Mr. Bull,

Colonel Henderson tells me you are writing a book on teddy bears. You may be interested to know that mine is thought to be the oldest in the world. This has been confirmed by Mr. Fordham of the Bethnal Green museum.

Sir Edward Bear Bart appeared on Blue Peter on 21st March. I enclose a press cutting from our local paper.

I remain yours faithfully
Elizabeth Rimer.

to celebrate the fortieth birthday of Winnie-the-Pooh. His mother was guest of honor instead.

That was perhaps more appropriate, for it was really she who started the whole thing. The late Robert Pitman, a distinguished British journalist who had studied the whole thing pretty thoroughly, came out with an enlightening article in the *Sunday Express* of June 26, 1966:

> One day forty-six years ago a pretty young woman went into Harrods and bought a Teddy Bear for her son's first birthday. The bear had an astonishing future in front of it. . . .
>
> In 1920 A. A. Milne was thirty-eight and his wife Daphne about ten years younger. He was a successful play-wright, modest, gentle, bubbling with a quiet stream of bizarre humour. This humour, we are told, began to flow round the fat furry shape of the gift from Harrods.
>
> One day young Christopher Robin Milne came down from the nursery when the whimsical actor-manager Sir Nigel Playfair was there. In a gruff voice the boy said: "What a Funny Man. What a Funny Red Face." But he denied saying the words himself. He said it was his toy bear, whom he called Pooh, speaking.
>
> Thus Pooh came to life, along with the boy's other toys, a piglet (bought by friends), a stuffed donkey, a tiger. Adult visitors, when invited, would ask: "I suppose Pooh will be there?" Milne started writing about Pooh. His wife has recalled: "We were all acting little incidents with Pooh and the nursery animals the whole time . . . we were all quite idiotic about it. The animals had become very important to us."
>
> Mrs. Milne says they had fun in their world of very special intimacy, laughing at ridiculous jokes and "talking in our own special language. Looking back to those days I always see Pooh and the small boy with whom we shared

Mary with her little bear behind.

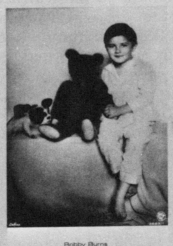

Bobby Burns

BIRTHDAY GREETINGS.

Teddy, Golly & Me

"Hurrah" for the
merican Eagle.
That beautiful
ird so hale;
Whom nobody
can inveigle.
r put Salt on
his lovely tail.

What ! Come Home ?
Not likely, when I'm at
Reading !

SUNDAY

FRIDAY

BEAR AND
FOR BEAR

Here's something to love
        and something to tease,
Something to cuddle and something
        to squeeze,

Someone
  who'll stick thro' storm and fair,
A dear little, cute little
        Brown Teddy Bear.

H.B. London, W.C.   Fully Protected.

MONDAY

SATURDAY

TUESDAY

BEAR AND
FOR BEAR

DINNERTIME.
While the other dollies wait
Teddy climbs into the plate.

"You'll be sorry when I'm gone."   "Vous allez vous ennuyer quand je serai partie."

WEDNESDAY

BEAR AND
FOR BEAR

THURSDAY

BEAR AND
FOR BEAR

LOOK AND SEE
WHAT "TEDDY" BEARS.

From
Margate

Registered.

him . . . with his large brown eyes and beautiful corn-coloured hair cut square."

"Yet is this the whole story?" asks Mr. Pitman, and proceeds to show us the other side of the coin — that is, what Christopher Robin himself really thought of it all. Mr. Pitman quotes from an article called "Father," which Christopher wrote in 1952, when he was thirty-two:

> Strangely enough, though my father wrote so much about me, he did not like children . . . in fact, he had as little to do with children as possible. I was his only child and I lived upstairs with my nanny. I saw very little of him. It was my mother who used to come and play in the nursery with me and tell him about the things I thought and did. It was she who provided most of the material for my father's books. As far as I can remember I knew nothing of the stories until they were published. Then my nanny used to read them to me. . . .

Was the son being fair to his father? We know that as he grew older the boy hated the idea of being the Christopher Robin of the stories and constantly being teased at school about his Teddy Bear. Yet he was clearly fond of his father and made him out to be a kind, delightful, and original man. As Christopher Robin commented in his article:

> Once, he found me sitting at a table with a fork upright. Instead of saying *that* isn't the correct way to hold a fork, he merely remarked: 'I shouldn't do it that way if I were you. If someone fell through the ceiling, they'd fall on to the prongs and that would hurt them.'

It seemed to Pitman that it was Mrs. Milne who got the most fun out of it all:

114

'My husband dictated the stories to me. I didn't type or anything, but he needed an audience to react. He would walk to and fro, puffing at his pipe while I wrote and laughed.'

. . . One thinks of . . . A. A. Milne [saying] about his [own] writing . . . that it was never sentimental, that all the characters in Pooh are in fact selfish and tough as nails, that even the little boy in Christopher Robin saying his prayers is actually as egocentric and unfettered by morals as any other young animal. Were these stories written primarily for a child at all? Or were they in fact written for the delight of the child's mother? It is an ironic thought. But then, in children's stories, irony and success seem to trip onwards hand in hand. The original Alice became estranged from Lewis Carroll, and Kenneth Grahame's adored son, who had the blessing of first hearing *The Wind in the Willows*, took his own life when still in his teens.

Perhaps there is a sadness in the Pooh stories, the sense of a dream existence poised uncertainly on the edge of the harsh world which has helped to make them immortal.

So much for Christopher Robin! Now what happened to Pooh? In 1947 Elliott Macrae, the president of Dutton, arranged to transport to the United States the original playthings which had inspired the books. Insured for $50,000, Piglet, Eeyore, Tigger, and Kanga crossed the Atlantic and then started traveling across the continent on a nationwide tour. They were introduced at a tea given by Macy's stores and received similar immense attention at the libraries, bookshops, and vast emporiums they visited. The animals are now safely ensconced in the reception room of E. P. Dutton and Company at 201 Park Avenue South, and there they receive visitors from all over the world.

In 1961 Dr. Alexander Lennard produced *Winnie Ille Pu*, a Latin translation of the classic described by the *New York Herald Tribune*

Me and my muff

This little bear climbed the Matterhorn
This little bear sat still
These little bears did nothing
And this little bear had a frill

as "the status book of the year." It took the author seven years to write the book, as he had to work his way through the Messrs. Juvenal, Pliny, and Ovid to find sentences to fit. But over a hundred thousand copies were sold before you could say "Julius Caesar." It was only the other day that somebody noticed a copy on the Archbishop of Canterbury's drawing room table.

In the Russian version the hero is called Vinni-Pukh. He has learned a kind of halting Russian to match his halting English and has moved from the wonderful forest to the "taiga." He's become the favorite of millions of Soviet children, to whom the word for Teddy Bear has always been Mishka. The translator, Boris Zakhoder, explains Pooh's new name to his readers: "Kristofer Robin knew a swan in a pond whose name was Pukh, a most suitable name for a swan [swansdown in Russian is "Pukh"] and if you call a swan loudly 'Pukh Pukh' and he does not answer, you can always pretend you were making gun noises just for fun. Anyhow, Kristofer's swan disappeared, so he named his bear Pukh so that his name wouldn't be forgotten."

Zakhoder is at his ingenious best with English words that have a double meaning in Russian. For instance, the Russian word for "discover" also means "open" (otkryt). Vinni thus thinks the North Pole is a box to be opened, not a place to discover. *Vinni-Pukh i Vse-Vse-Vse* (And all-all-all) is one of the most successful children's books to appear in Russia in the last decade; 358,000 copies have been printed, there have been Vinni-Pukh puppets and TV shows, and untold millions of children have rechristened their Mishkas "Vinni."

The Pooh cult has become so intense and so personal that I suppose it isn't surprising the Disney film came in for such devastating criticism. The addition of a fresh character (a gopher), allegedly to help the American market, infuriated aficionados, and on April 16, 1966 there was a fierce attack in London's *Daily Mail*, which stated that "in the very Unenchanted Forest of film commerce, a gopher is worth more than a Piglet." The latter was cut clean out of the film, Mr. Wolfgang Reithermann, the director, claiming that there was simply

no *room* for him. Mr. R had apparently never heard of Pooh until 1961! and furthermore, he rather unwisely announced that "as far as Pooh is concerned, we stayed closer to the original than we'd ever done on anything before."

The rights to Pooh had fallen into Mr. Disney's hands on June 16, 1961, and for the next three years, a director, six writers, eleven animators, nine "voices," three background artists, four layout designers, and two composers rewrote, redrew, and resang the Milne books. All told, a hundred and fifty Disney men were involved: all this for a twenty-six minute film called *Winnie the Pooh and the Honey Tree*! One trace of the British original does remain but only in the version shown in the old country. This is the voice of Christopher Robin; it was amended only after a brave stand by the film critic of the *Evening News*, Felix Barker, who couldn't bear hearing Christopher Robin speak with an American accent. He dispatched a fusillade of cables to Hollywood, with the result that the boy's voice was redubbed.

Disney had apparently been worried by "the Britishness" of the original. Said Mr. Reithermann: "The Midwest accent, in which all the characters speak, is the general neutral accent, acceptable to the whole American market."

In the Ernest Shephard drawings, which are such a delightful feature of the books, Christopher Robin has long hair and wears a smock, but as one of the American animators, Mr. Hal King, put it: "Christopher Robin came out too *sissified*. So we gave him a haircut and some decent clothes." He came out looking like Pinocchio! I think perhaps this is the moment to report that a "Winnie-the-Pooh" drawing by Shephard was recently sold at Sotheby's for twelve hundred pounds. How much do original Hal Kings fetch?

I cannot conclude this sad history of Pooh's trip into the film world without a word about the lyrics supplied for his use. The nuttiness of Milne's songs had alarmed the filmmakers, and the Brothers Sherman (Oscar winners and all that!) were imported to devise an entirely fresh lot. And here they are side by side. Hmph!

A. A. Milne	The Sherman Brothers
It's a very funny thought that, if Bears were Bees They'd build their nests at the BOTTOM of trees. And that being so (if the Bees were Bears) We shouldn't have to climb up all those stairs.	*Winnie-the-Pooh, Winnie-the-Pooh, Tubby little cubby all stuffed with fluff. He's Winnie-the-Pooh, Winnie-the-Pooh, Willy Nilly Silly ole bear.*

And hmph again!

Perhaps one day a film worthy of Pooh will be made. Meanwhile, one thing is certain: his appeal remains totally undiminished. The explanation? Well, the chief buyer for the biggest toy shop in London put it rather succinctly when yet again he found himself sold out of models of Mr. Milne's creations.

"I can only put it down to the kids' wanting to be with it," he announced.

A World of Its Own

Dear God thank you for the bees that make the honey, and for my mistress who takes such good care of me. Please don't let her throw me away or give me to someone else," wrote seven-year-old Janet Dinnie on behalf of her Teddy Bear (in a book by Jane Deverson called *An Octopus in My Head*).

It would be very difficult for the Almighty to resist such a petition. Teddies are so often uppermost in children's thoughts at the end of the day when blessings are counted that this sort of prayer must now seem very ordinary to Him. In some cases, a whole world is peopled almost entirely with Teddies. And with a lively imagination and a warm heart what a world it can be!

Take the Teddy Bear world of Miss Jeanne Becker for example:

> *For many years I had a large family of bears, of varying sizes and colours, family tree attached. Most important was Tina (originally Tiny in contrast to her sister Big), my first bear. At one time she was styled Queen of the Fairies. Her influence was recognised by adults, for instance when my grandmother gave us ten shillings (we are three girls) there was always sixpence for Tina.*
>
> *She suffered severely at my hands. Her original eyes I pulled out and my mother replaced these with red wooden beads. Then a girl friend told me that Tina's fur would grow again if I cut it off. It never did!*
>
> *My classmates treated her with scant respect and once when we seven- and eight-year-olds were taken by teachers to spend a week studying the countryside, the two girls with whom I shared a bedroom played ball with Tina! But looking after the bears was a serious matter for me:*

123

the very small ones wore skirts and hats embroidered in cross stitch: I even sat sewing on the beach during our annual holiday in the Isle of Wight. The toys travelled in my younger sister's empty pram. They had school note-books and outings. At home they lived in a corner cup-board called Toy Hotel. The ground floor of Toy Hotel was a shop, run by Tina's handsome husband, Oberon Bruin. When it opened, the advertising ran something like this: "I haven't got any decent clothes," with the answer: "Go to Bruin's, then, you silly."

As the bears graduated to the rank of fairy they were given girdles of finely plaited embroidery silk. There were several weddings (marriages of twins and brothers and sisters were allowed, as the expense of buying outside stock was too heavy) and births (rather fanciful, with ba-bies dropping from above, having to be caught by the doc-tor, who happened to be Horace Horsecollar).

Tina came with me to Paris when I spent a year there studying. She also visited Italy and Switzerland, and flew to Puerto Rico to meet my nieces. Here she had a royal welcome from a committee of toys of the two genera-tions (i.e., my sister's and her girls'). She had a special dress made for the occasion out of remnants of material from a dress made for my older niece.

Then Tina changed her style of dress, favouring slacks and a chunky-knit cardigan. My nephews were al-lowed to play with her, gently, and last Christmas when I was away Tina spent the holidays with them. During this time she fell in love with Adi, a rather bad-tempered-looking German bear, of roughly the same vintage, and wanted to stay. A wedding was therefore held: as a result the boys commissioned new suits of clothes for all their bears. I laid out my remnants and priced them: however, the shop was raided and a police report had to be made (how different from the sedate games I used to invent in the 1930's!).

Recently Tina had a baby, a very realistic setting this time.

Miss Becker turned out to be a regular correspondent. Here is an extract from one of her letters:

"Our little lot are recovering from a session with anti-tank artillery! And now I've been commissioned to make a BATMAN mask and cloak for a small junior bear. Can't keep up with their sartorial requirements, but luckily they often forget. . . ."

Most of the inhabitants of Miss Becker's bear world have vanished, but Tina is still going very strong. She was last heard of leaving for Puerto Rico again in a long-sleeved mini, as her legs are still pretty good, though her arms are ready for surgery. She had in her luggage some new pink linen sheets with pillowslip to match, all embossed with the initial T.

In the last chapter I had occasion to refer to a letter I'd received from the president of the Sydney University Tiddlywinks Society. At first I thought it was all a bit fishy but later I entered into a fairly regular correspondence with David Frankel, who turned out to be a genuine arctophilist of the highest caliber. Both he and his sister gave me a glimpse of their Teddy Bear world — a world even more royal than Miss Becker's.

During the Reign of the Bears the Frankel family were living in South Africa, and David wrote to me first about the lineage which they had traced to way back before he and Theresa were thought of.

Golden Bear owned me and Teddy owned my sister.
of Royal Lineage. King Koala Bear (1856 – 1872) succeeded
by King Black Bear (1872 – 1908) King Timothy Bear
(1908 – 1924) and Kings Golden and Teddy (1940 –   )
All the Bears had birthdays every month and our two both
celebrated theirs on the 27th.

In 1956 the bears had crowns and red cloaks with
ermine edgings (cotton wool with ink blobs actually). It is
odd that my and my sister Theresa's two bears came to the
throne in 1940, as neither of us were born then.

125

Busy Buzzy

The Frankel bears at their studies

Royal or not, our bears had bills to pay and post office accounts and indeed banks. An old exercise book yields the information that Teddy and Golden Bear paid fifteen shillings and sixpence for water and light bills (this was of course before decimal currency overtook South Africa). Golden Bear had thirty-five shillings in the bank, deposited in two separate lots, one of one pound five shillings and one a month later of ten shillings. Teddy Bear, by some strange coincidence, had the same amount deposited and on the same days. My sister and I conducted a series of transactions and even withdrew money from the accounts (my sister to pay a debt of ten shillings to a Mr. Nicholas Monkey).

In the old exercise book there is a fascinating invitation to "Teddy's Coronation" which reads as follows: "To Mommy. You are invitat to the Teddy's Coronation. To be held in the big Room. Strait after lunch."

Theresa Frankel, under pressure, was able to supply a little additional information: "We used books of Malta lottery tickets for checkbooks and a post office set which I was given as a present. . . . I'm not really sure of David's and my position in Teddy Bear Land. I suppose we were sort of Grand Viziers and State Veterinary Surgeons."

There you have it: a boy and his sister sharing a bear world happily. A lady born in Wabash County during the Depression has told me that she and her sister lived in a separate world which made them completely unaware of parental problems until their father walked out on them. The most important thing to them were their two (each) Teddies. Hers were called Cubby and Hubby and her sister's Teddy and Stubby. She reports that they always treated the quartet "with the utmost love and respect" and she is certain that the bears, in return, helped them to survive the desertion of their father and taught them "to live with little and enjoy much."

Years later, when my correspondent became a nurse, her training conflicted with her personal judgment. "Stuffed toys are great carriers of pin-worm eggs" was a dictum dished out to her, with which she had perforce to agree. Yet she feels that Teddy Bear attachments are far too valuable for considerations of hygiene ! Incidentally, by some curious deduction which she doesn't explain, she attributes some of her family's conversion to Catholicism entirely to the influence of the bears.

Which brings us to the alarming theory that your bear should be of your own faith. But ought you to impose this in a supposedly free world? Perhaps my own little Theodore is thinking this very moment of "going over" to the Greek Orthodox Church, as he spends so much time in a country where it holds so much sway.

Of course, some bears actually go into the Church. Like the Archdeacon of the Marshes. You haven't heard of him? Well, he is just about the most original and mature Teddy I have ever come across and I am indebted to Winifred Seaton of Colchester for letting me know all about him.

Our family's bear is rather unusual but you will find his story of some interest especially in view of his great age and because of the effect he has had on human beings. Please bear in mind that in all other respects we are a perfectly ordinary family: my brother a Classics master at a very well-known public school; my sister married to an irrigation adviser to the Colonial Office; and myself a teacher of older children.

Buzzy* claims to be the oldest Teddy Bear "alive." He is sixty-four. In 1905 he was given to my brother on his second or third birthday. We were then living in Germany, as my father was British chaplain at Bad Homburg. Because of his size my brother hardly ever played with him then and my sister and I, who were a few years older, each had a small one. Years later when we were almost grown up Buzzy was brought out for a charade and never put away again.

*Buzzy the Archdeacon was the inspiration of a charming book called "Buzzy" by F. E. Mecklin, published over forty years ago. It was dedicated to "Those other friends of mine who live with Buzzy."

Gradually, as he sat about the place, he became part of the family — with decided views on all family matters. He in fact smoothed over frictions when they arose. By this time we had moved to England and my father was the rector of a Norfolk parish. Here stories grew up around the bear. We learned that he had a "Cure" of rabbits in the fields around the Rectory. He later became Archdeacon of the Marshes. Letters addressed to him, as they often were, naturally caused some embarrassment to my father.

Once we found in the Eastern Daily Press *a letter from the parson of a neighbouring small town (a pompous little man) thanking friends for their congratulations on his having been made a Rural Dean but assuring them that he was* not *the Archdeacon of the Marshes. (A letter of course had gone astray but all our friends who knew the bear knew, too, for whom the letter had been meant.) "I shall never be able to face X again if he gets to know the truth," said my poor father.*

Only once did we have a family holiday without taking the bear with us. He spent the time in the house of some Roman Catholic friends, "went over to Rome," and was unfrocked. Later he joined the fishing fleet but soon after war came was discharged, on account of flat feet, so he said! He is proud of the medals which he wears but it is hard to know why he got them.

There were, of course, during his long life, occasions when he actually took part *in events. Once he was smiled on by royalty, once he came up against the law, and once he was found by my father sitting on the drawing-room sofa with the rather austere Bishop. My father smoothed it over by referring to "children in the house" (there were of course none) and he told us this with some shame at having let the bear down — not the Church!*

Miss Seaton has told me of certain physical changes which the Archdeacon has had to undergo. A certain readjustment of stuffing was deemed necessary at one time: "Kapok is, I think, and always has been the chief ingredient, but he has had a number of major operations during his long life and those include not only Kapok transfusions but regrafting of fur from the limbs to the face, an entirely satisfactory operation, leaving no disfigurement at all."

Buzzy and Theodore have now become Pen Pals, and in a recent dispatch Miss Seaton comments: "The Archdeacon is most sympathetic with Theodore about the Greek lessons but a little anxious over the fast set of bears he's mixing with. Not censorious at all, remembering his own young days and his hurried marriage to the charming little white bear, Julia. How grateful he was to my father for performing the ceremony so that the triplets were born in wedlock, particularly as the whole affair coincided with his appointment as Archdeacon."

After a broadcast talk I did on the BBC, Buzzy was swift to take umbrage. The news reached me fast. "I was awoke by a telephone call: 'Peter Bull on the wireless about bears.' I listen all agog. Not a word. Not a whisper about me. Theodore will feel for me my shame."

I wrote a letter of apology, and a generous reply followed:

> *That was a very kind letter. I think that bears are quick to feel things and often take umbrage that they should not take. Old as I am, there are times I would dearly love to be on tele. I was so glad you called me "Buzzy" as all my friends do.*

It's a world of its own!

133

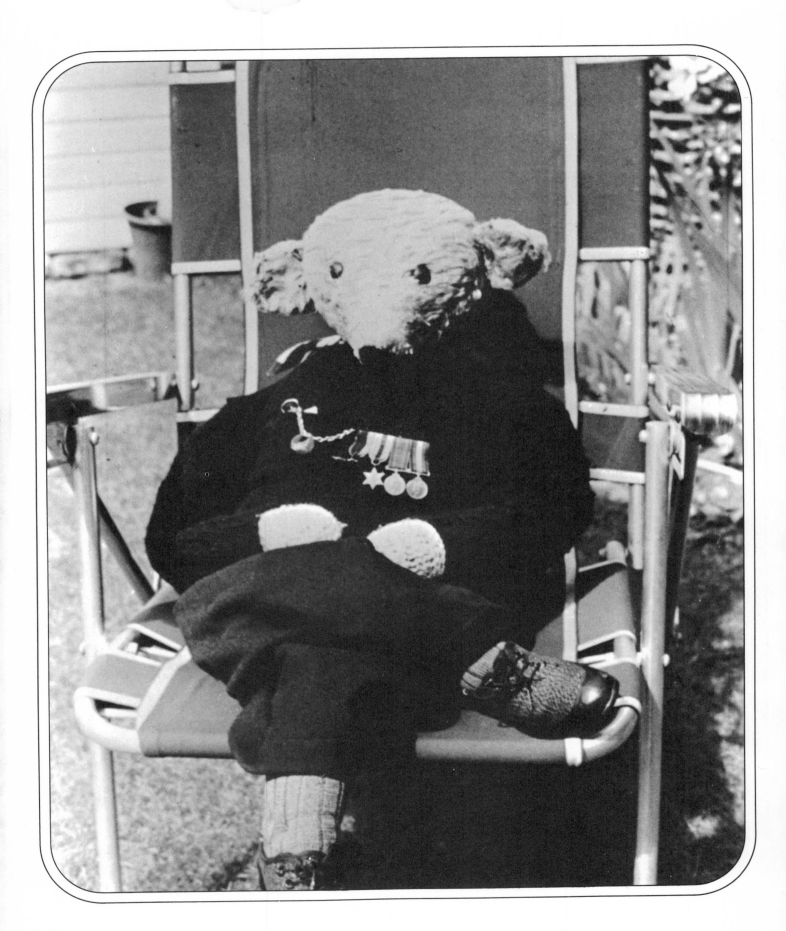

Full Dress

Go to sleep, my Teddy Bear,
Close your little button eyes,
And let me smooth your hair.
It feels so soft and silky that,
I'd love to cuddle down by you,
So,
*Go to sleep, my darling Teddy Bear.**

It is astonishing how large a part the wardrobe plays in the fantasy world of Teddy and his owner. Some people feel very strongly about what should be worn and what should not be worn. It is, for instance, unlikely that the above-mentioned Teddy would have gone to sleep in ready-made pajamas. Most owners like to invent clothes or have them made by an indulgent adult. Wendy Boston, who manufactures the animals by the thousands in England, once produced an already pajamaed Teddy. He flopped on the market. The general verdict was that he looked too human. Most people like to start with their Teddy bare, and gradually give him individual costuming and props.

There has always been great rivalry among girls, their sisters, and "best friends" for sartorial elegance in their dolls, but Teddies, I'll have you know, come in for equal attention. A Mrs. Childs of South Ligonier, Pennsylvania, takes it one step further and tells us about a feud between two nannies, hers from Ireland and her "best friend's" from Scotland.

They competed to see who could make the best clothes for our Teddies. If Bridie made pyjamas, then Jessie made pyjamas, and so on. But alas, one day the contest was over; my Teddy appeared in a white linen suit with lapels, a white shirt, a necktie, and a belt with a little silver buckle. As if that weren't enough, he had a top coat made in a hounds-tooth check with a silk lining and real pockets.

*Fairly old lullaby

Not only did the nurses not speak over that but my *best friend was so jealous that she hardly spoke to* me *for days. The only ones that seemed not to care one bit about the whole affair were the two Teddies.*

Some owners experiment to improve their Teddies' looks or well-being. Johnny Pitt, an old naval chum of mine, emptied an entire bottle of brilliantine over his animal's head to make the hair grow again. The results were, I fear, unsuccessful and very smelly. The same long-suffering bear was called up into the army (World War I) and wore a complete khaki uniform with buttons of gold sealing wax, impressed with a seal from a real army button.

Miss Thonger got very worried about her bear's not having enough to eat. He was fifteen inches high and colored deep rose-pink. Miss T also had a blue-clad pixie-doll—but she wasn't remotely keen on it, thank goodness. The latter's "roguishly cheerful expression" upset her equilibrium and caused its own downfall. For Miss Thonger used to carve it up daily with a wooden penknife and feed the fragments to the bear. Even at the time (she was five) she admitted it was rather a rotten thing to do but she felt that her Teddy needed the nourishment. It was simply no good her elder sister's assuring her that bears were not meat eaters. She couldn't and indeed didn't believe her.

I must say I think some people take terrific chances the way they treat their bears. Miss Thonger genuinely believed her Teddy to be on a different plane from a mere doll, but there is a danger in trying to make him into something he doesn't really want to be.

"I think Teddy is so well preserved because he has never been dragged about or suffered the indignities of being dressed like a doll." So wrote Mrs. Lavender Russell of her fifty-year-old friend who was born in the Army and Navy Stores in Calcutta. He now lives quietly in London, but in his youth he was quite a seasoned traveler. He sailed on the maiden voyage of the *Queen of Bermuda* and later went to the Far East in the troopship *Empire Orwell.*

Teddy remained in my bunk, where he could look through the porthole. He appeared to take a great interest in Gibraltar, Suez, Colombo, and finally Singapore, where he lived with us for three hot, sticky years. He is now a shade of silver-mink (he was a pale mushroom-brown), and has little or no fur on his head. The sad loss of an eye has given him a knowing and rakish look. He has nobbly marks on his hands and feet where moths or cockroaches got at him once. His ears make faint papery noises when pinched, and that is all that is left of his squeaks.

But Mrs. Russell prefers him to any silly old doll!

There is no doubt about the contempt that Teddy owners feel about dolls. This animosity was for some reason particularly pronounced at the beginning of the century. "I had a dozen of them," writes Mrs. Freestone from the Isle of Wight, "but I never cared for them. I used to deck them out in beads, and Teddy and I, as bandits, used to stalk them round the sofa and hold them up to ransom."

Her Teddy was operated on by her father, who performed a "Growlectomy," but he survived long enough to make an incoming dachshund so jealous that he, Teddy, had to be "laid away in lavender." But now, at the ripe age of sixty, he's back on Mrs. Freestone's bed, "staring at her with his little boot button eyes."

I must get this button-eye business straight. So many of the older generation refer to "shoe buttons." There must be some radical difference. A Brooklyn man had shoe buttons on his, but then his Teddy was unusual to start with. He was constructed entirely out of red flannel by the mother, who could not afford a ready-made one. You see, the boy was the youngest of seven children.

A plea for some glass eyes came from the owner of an emigrant bear who doesn't care for the black wool ones which somebody had improvised for him. After life at a boarding school in London ("couldn't have survived the place without him") and the Blitz ("nothing worse than bits of plaster in his fur"), he is now thirty-five years old and lives in California, with the wool pulled over his eyes.

Teddy's eyes have always been a bone of contention in the nursery. They are a potential source of danger to the Very Young, because, even if properly inserted, they can break from their shanks and be swallowed. The Hospital for Sick Children in London says that over the years "there have been several cases of children swallowing glass eyes from Teddy Bears, but we are happy to say that this has never reached alarming proportions."

I have put our friend with the woolen peepers in touch with Miss Mendenhall of Duluth, Minnesota, who launders bears, restores eyes, embroiders noses, and puts on new chamois paws. Her own Teddy is still her favorite possession (she sent me an enchanting bookplate of him lying on his tummy reading; he is apparently a prolific reader).

Miss Mendenhall repairs for pleasure, but Mrs. Leggett ("late of Alum Rock Road," as it says on her brochure) does it professionally. I have included her letter in full because in these haphazard days it's a delight to find someone so sensitive and painstaking in a business which has practically gone to the dogs. She writes from the Dolls' Hospital and Beauty Parlour in Erdington Market, England, whose claims are: "Every make of doll repaired. Nylon wigs that wash and comb. Clothes to fit every make of doll including Cindy, Tessy, Paul, Tiny Tears, and old-fashioned dolls. Shoes, socks, hats, coats, etc. Teddy Bears and soft toys repaired and cleaned. No job too big—none too small. Open every Tuesday, Friday, and Saturday."

We have cleaned and repaired hundreds over the years [writes Mrs. Leggett]. *Some you would have thought should be put in the dustbin. There was a little boy going on his holidays to Ireland. When the family was ready Paul had his tattered Teddy under his arm. Dad says you're not taking that thing with you on the plane, he said I am, if Teddy isn't going I'm not. So they both went. Then there was this little fellow put his Teddy up on the counter. I said what's his complaint. He said I want a set of pyjamas for him. He sleeps with me and I think he should have pyjamas so we fitted him up another satisfied customer. Then there was the little girl who said when you put Teddy's leg on don't give him the needle. Then there was the two little girls brought dolls and teddies for repair. When my assistant gave them the ticket and told them what they would cost they said oh? have you to pay? They said they thought it was a hospital and you could get it on the National Health. Then finally there was the two little girls that stood by the stall for about half an hour as we were packing up for going home. I said did you want something love? No. Are you waiting for Mummie? No. Waiting for your folks? No. Well what are you waiting for? We are waiting to see the ambulances come to take away the Dolls and Teddies. For once I was struck for an answer. After quick thinking I said Oh the ambulance won't be here for a couple of hours. I should come some other day. I couldn't tell them they were all packed away in cartons and going in an ordinary car. Well I hope you get as much fun from your book as we get dealing with the children. It is heartbreaking work sometimes but we love it and perhaps you'll be surprised to know I am seventy-five years young. My husband who does the doll repairs is seventy-nine and my friend who does the Teddies is seventy-four. One of my dressmakers is seventy-four and the "ambulance driver" is sixty-eight. . . . We are the only Dolls' Hospital in Birmingham so you can imagine we are kept pretty busy.*

I got this letter over three years ago, so you can work out the astonishing longevity of Mrs. Leggett and her staff *now*. I only hope they are still at it. My friend Mr. Kent, above whom I have lived so long and happily in the King's Road, Chelsea, has been running his Dolls' Hospital for many years. He used to have an enchanting notice in his window which read: "Wigs Fitted to Any Doll."

But I don't intend to get mixed up with the doll world at this juncture, a feeling I know Mrs. Fowler of London will share with me. She has no time for them either. Listen! "When the first World War

Served in Burma

Served in World War I

Served double purpose in bed

Teddy Bare

broke out and everyone sprang into uniform, an honorary aunt made my dissolute Teddy Bear a Highland suit, complete with sporran. He must have looked idiotic but I loved him."

There was an influx of Japanese dolls at the time ("they all wore kimonos with rather nasty, cheap underclothes") which she didn't approve of, and then, to top it all off, she was given a Fairy at some Rich Child's Party of which there were plenty in those days ("with real Nannies standing round the walls," reports Mrs. F with relish).

She heaps scorn on the doll: "She was breathtakingly lovely, but after you'd admired her spangles for a day or two, there was nothing you could *do* with her. Her dress wouldn't come off and even if it had, she wouldn't have been a fairy any more. So pride of place was still Teddy's. You could make him into anything, bash him about, give him any part and he'd play it. You could even operate on him in the dolls' hospital, provided some obliging grownup sewed him up again."

Teddies quite often have tummy troubles, in any case, and are inured to this sort of thing. Mrs. Hoffman of Connecticut told me about Brownie, who has been a very chic bear all his life. His wardrobe was tailored mainly in Paris, and in 1963 Mr. and Mrs. H accompanied him an extra five hundred miles in Europe so as to hold his hand while he was undergoing a stomach operation, to say nothing of a skin-lift, at Steiff's factory in Giengen. There he became such a favorite that everything was done free of charge. However, there is always a cloud popping out through those silver linings, and apparently he has grown very stout since the "op" and can't get into any of his old fitted clothes.

Unlike a London bear of over sixty years who now has to wear a knitted suit to cover his rather bare tummy and slimmer waistline, induced by loss of stuffing. Otherwise, however, he's sound of wind and limb, has his original eyes and "his old sweet expression" in spite of the fact that the soles of his feet and palms of his hands have been renewed with pieces of an old uncle's vest.

Somebody who has never had any tummy trouble is Old Ted Moore. He is of a species long since extinct, with a tummy which opened with hooks and eyes and held a pint-sized hot-water bottle under his fur. He has had a rich full life — a stint, among other things, in World War I dressed up as a wounded soldier to collect money on flag days. Later he was persuaded to sit in his owner's hair-dressing establishment to reassure the younger clientele. He is now well over sixty and a well-known local figure. When, recently, he was stolen by a small girl who hid him in her pram, her mother luckily recognized him and restored him to his rightful owner.

I have a feeling that Old Ted is far too active to contemplate spending any time in the Teddy Bear Club, where old and respected members of the breed can spend the evening of their lives in peace. As yet a small organization (there are only five members but they are all in their sixties), it is, I am ashamed to say, a branch of the Sussex, England, Doll Club. But it works in conjunction with the Teddy Bear Preservation Society, which has its own headquarters. Naturally!

And what stories those five could tell! And probably do, endlessly to each other. But then most Teddy Bears seem to lead frightfully interesting lives. Just mention the animal's mere name to somebody: reminiscence will follow reminiscence and the most unlikely people will confess to a secret life which for some unknown reason they've kept under dust sheets since childhood.

Sometimes the effect will be practical and the animals will benefit from their owner's sense of guilt and be taken from some attic or trunk and restored to favor.

"I think I'll clean them up and put them back in my room," wrote Miss Marilyn Franconero from New Jersey, adding in a sudden burst of loyalty: "If I ever saved one thing I know it would be them."

But it isn't enough just to *have* a bear; a lot of owners consider it essential that the bears be up to date in their attire. One British dowager, who received a Teddy from America in 1906, has other views on the subject:

> *He had two costumes, a pink striped cotton dress*
> *which I thought very unsuitable and transferred to one of*

143

my dolls, and blue cotton overalls, as worn in America, with "Teddy B" (Teddy Bad) embroidered on them. The dress represented "Teddy G" (Teddy Good). I always understood that the bears were named after Teddy Roosevelt, which makes the dress seem even more irrelevant.

The lady obviously objected to her Teddy's being in workman's rig and it is true that they rarely appear in anything but the smartest garb. Even class distinction is apt to creep into this world: a lady sent me a photograph of her family of ten with the comment: "You can see that they are definitely not common bears but real gentry."

Another snap showed a Teddy in full hunting kit, designed by a famous American couturier. This well-pawed animal had an extensive wardrobe ranging from Scots kilts to sun suits (he winters in Florida) and being "essentially a sailor at heart, he has the usual foul-weather gear."

His owner, deprived of her original bear by an unsympathetic mother (yes, again!) who donated him to the Salvation Army, has certainly lavished love on his successor. "I'm sure all my friends think I'm round the bend when they see me making a blue-checked summer wardrobe (monogrammed of course) and knitting pullovers and cardigans for Bear and his playmate, who is but one inch high."

Sometimes a Teddy captivates his owner by some physical peculiarity or even deformity. A New York lady had a childhood friend who was lopsided, had a yarn nose, a yarn mouth, and yarn eyes. One leg, one arm, and one eye were all smaller than the other and yet he was always the hero in her fantasies. Usually she was the princess and Teddy the handsome slave whom she rescued from bondage (ancient Egyptian setting). Or else she reversed their roles and he was a pirate and she was a captive slave whom *he* rescued. Her bed was the ship. "Afterwards he stayed awake to protect me while I slept," she ends. "P.S. I loved him."

There is no doubt that every Teddy owner believes in the protective powers of his or her chum. Even when real animals are involved. I know a family where a Great Dane, long resident, didn't know what had hit her when the son and heir deserted her almost completely for a new Teddy Bear. Up till then she'd regarded herself as Queen of the Household. A few years later she fell ill and couldn't move about and the small boy took his Teddy down and lay him by the bed so that she wouldn't be lonely. What the Great Dane thought of this isn't recorded but I suspect that she made a speedy recovery.

Children don't understand why a relationship with a Teddy is apt to be so much more rewarding than with an animal, but it is easy for *us* to see why. Teddies don't mind being taken for a walk, beaten about, dressed in ridiculous hats (at least they don't complain *aloud!*), or even being read to. There are no jealousies or other emotional upheavals to contend with — no pressure, no guilt. And not only do Teddies seem to be more *satisfactory* to get involved with than real animals, but there are also cases of their even superseding humans entirely because of their qualities. A lady from Detroit confessed to me that she recalls more about her bear in 1918 than she does about her sister. "It's a strange and awful thing to say. But then if you'd had a huge dark red-plush Teddy with eyes that lighted up, I think you'd find that he'd make a pretty deep impression on you at an early age."

Sometimes these impressions of the very young can be revived by outside influences. After hearing me on the radio, Mrs. Bridget Wastre wrote:

> *How odd that a word spoken or written can stir up a whole host of recollections. You speak of Theodore's eyes. Now I remember well my brother some forty years ago sucking at the lovely limpid yellow pools with a dark centre which were my Teddy's eyes. My grandmother had a little maid (two shillings and sixpence a week and her keep all 'round) who removed Teddy's eyes and sewed buttons in their place. As to his height I would say he is a compact eighteen inches and I wish you could see how beautifully his arms are curved. His coat is now a lovely*

faded camel colour but it was a rich gold if one looks in the creases of his legs (not the yellow brassy gold of Teds today but what my mother called old gold). I wonder, if we had an "autopsy" and restored his "growler" would proof of his true origin come to light? Though it would break my heart to have him vivisected by a modern Dolls' Hospital.

Mrs. Wastre pronounces her Theodore THE MOST FAMOUS BEAR OF ALL, and although I cannot agree with her (nor indeed can my Theodore), she certainly has some claim to the title. He belonged originally to her sister, who was the goddaughter of a famous actress of the Edwardian era, Rosina Dowson, who appeared before Theodore Roosevelt at the beginning of the century. The President presented her with a Teddy, which she brought home as a gift to Mrs. Wastre's sister.

Eventually he passed into Mrs. W's possession and now sits in a "Lloyds loom chair with Fenella, a doll I made for my daughter, and a tarty little cutie I won at St. Giles's Fair when I was a child." And Mrs. W, one feels, would come down pretty hard on anyone who'd dare try to pinch him.

It's the same old story: the fiercely protective quality which comes over an owner whose Teddy is in danger. A small boy, who couldn't swim, jumped into the English river Severn to save his bear friend from drowning. The boatman, who saved the boy, realized the value of the graying moth-eaten bear and rowed upstream to rescue him, too. Another small boy, named Graham White, fought a fire for twenty minutes to save two Teddy Bears. He didn't have time to dial "999" (the British "emergency" phone number). There was also a boy knocked down by a van who said "Teddy's hurt too" when the ambulance arrived.

These brave kids were absolutely certain that their Teddies were as real as they themselves were. We don't need a psychiatrist to tell us how the mere possession of something very dear can lead to acts of unselfishness and self-sacrifice. The advantages of living in a fan-

146

tasy world are legion. Most children would prefer not to share theirs with adults, but there are numerous examples where other people, particularly parents, are involved to a certain degree. This leads to elaborate inventions and pretenses. Mother is, on the whole, more liable to be available to share the make-believe than Father, who is off earning the daily bread. Yet Father is frequently coerced into playing a leading role, too, and there are even cases of his having to take Teddy to work, so that the latter can "help." This involves a certain number of reassuring phone calls during the day and bulletins have to be issued at intervals in the bear's voice.

I'm duty bound to say that I have never superimposed a voice on Theodore and at this late date I simply don't intend to. It is highly probable that he would give me my come-uppance if he suddenly found his powers of speech. Yet I do have conversations with him and they don't seem all that one-sided to me. You think that's odd? Listen! I know a lady of forty-five who waits till her husband has gone to the office and then pops up to the attic to have a long conversation about Life with *her* old Teddy.

Mary and her bear behind

The Bear Facts

It is sadly true that the modern Teddy Bear has little resemblance to the early ones. Even Steiff has made adjustments to models which seemed well-nigh perfection to me. Nowadays so-called fashionable bears wear a nylon fur coat which can be washed or brushed. A far cry from the lovely plush and velvet numbers filled with sawdust or wood shavings who looked as if they'd seen a bit of Life with a capital L! You can now have a Teddy made of foam rubber which can join you in the bath. There are battery-driven walking bears and even one with a built-in gyroscope which enables it to ride a tiny two-wheeled cycle. There are musical bears containing minute tape recorders which will croon "Happy Birthday" at you or shout out pithy remarks like "I want some honey" or "Kiss me." Others will yawn and stretch when a built-in alarm clock goes off. Perhaps my most unfavorite refinement of all is the transistor-driven tape which is hidden in the bear's head. You are supposed to press a button and say anything you like. Then you press another button and the bear's eyes light up and it (I can't bring myself to call him "he") repeats what you've told it, though the tiny loudspeaker is so adjusted that it deepens your voice into a growl. It's not advised, they say, to put *this* model in your bath.

I suppose some of you are saying: "What's he carrying on about? Only a few pages ago he was telling us about the 'Growler' and other unusual bears of the early nineteen hundreds. What's the difference?"

And the terrible thing is that I don't know whether I can explain, at least to your complete satisfaction. It's just that, in my opinion, there are certain special things in life which should never be changed. It's simply no good having a bear who gets in a bath with you (you know instinctively that They Hate Water) or one with a machine attached to him which may very well give you a nasty electric shock. Their very

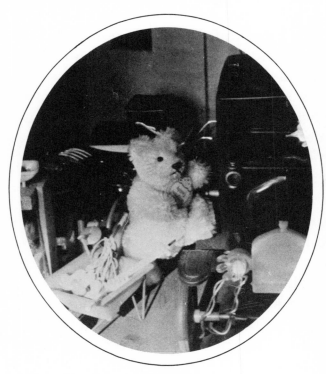

Miss Dinah Cody's bears are at home

modernity turns them into some slightly spooky animal who is neither one thing nor the other and of whom you can never be sure. You can't imagine them listening or just Being Quiet. Friendship would seem to be out of the question because in some way they attract all too much attention to themselves.

The basic security value in Teddies used to be that they never changed in their attitude toward you, and none of us older arctophilists can see the point in a bear who is too intent on being clever himself to see how clever we are being. And even the ones who are so brilliantly constructed mechanically have frightfully stupid faces. I've seen recently in shops Teddies, who should be ashamed of themselves, made of some wildly hygienic washable material, shining with smugness like plastic tablecloths, and about as friendly and lovable on the whole as hedgehogs with hepatitis.

But the fact remains that there has been no startling decline in the toy's popularity since the whole thing started. Manufacturers, I know, will try to prove that it's because they have moved with the times. And the ghastly thing is that they are very probably absolutely right. But I can't really believe that even the most sophisticated modern child is influenced by such appeals as are perpetrated by Wendy Boston Playsafe Toys at a store in Tunbridge Wells, England. "Please, Mummy, can we go to a shop where they've lots of lovely safe soft cuddly Wendy Boston Teddy Bears? They can go in the washing machine and through the spin dryer again and again and they last and last. They've got screwed-in nylon eyes that never come out and there's no nasty wire in them."

The main new colors for Teddy are shocking-pink, chartreuse, and orange. The original shade seems right out of fashion. Even the actual faces seem to have altered considerably. Yet, to be fair, I must admit that most of the biggest manufacturers of the toy insist that the basic benign appearance be adhered to. He must be furry, cuddly, and above all, friendly. A recent consignment arrived with eyes and mouth "at a menacing angle" and was sent back instantly.

But as long as there is a demand for Teddy as a companion, perhaps I shouldn't cavil too much at the March of Time. After all, sales are estimated at forty million dollars' worth in America alone, and despite the glut of Batmen, space rockets, killer-ray guns, and Kewpie dolls, it's a fair bet that Teddy will occupy the honored place on the average small pillow when bedtime comes.

A recent research project in America on the favorite toy for children proved a walk-over for our friend. Fifty-five percent named him as their choice. But as it is believed from another source that forty percent of purchased animals are bought by grownups for grownups, it is difficult to know where you really are.

Mrs. Hutchings supplies an enlightening report on the results of similar research she carried out in England upon overhearing a conversation on a bus which ended: "What *do* children play with now that they no longer like Teddy Bears?"

This sent shivers down her spine (she was about to embark on her delightful book at the time), and in 1963 she conducted her own census on Teddy Bears. Three hundred and fifty children from the age of five to eleven from every background were questioned; they, the guinea pigs, came from large and small towns, private, county, primary, or grammar schools.

Fifty were finally discarded because they were too old or too young, or obviously had been helped. Of the three hundred kids questioned (these were all from the British Isles) only thirty (i.e., ten percent) had no Teddy Bear: eighteen of these were boys and twelve girls. Of these, just over half came from a slum district where there was only TV and very little home life in the accepted sense of the word. In this particular area a great many of the children did not know what a Teddy Bear *was*. Every country child questioned, however, had one. Of the two hundred and seventy possessors, fifty-seven (twenty girls and thirty-seven boys) did not play with them. Most of these children were between nine and eleven years old, when you wouldn't expect a boy, at least, to be playing with a Teddy, or so says Mrs. Hutchings —and here I cross swords with her.

The younger boys and almost all the girls added that although

Lord Butler, once Chancellor of England, his sisters and their friends

they did not play with their bears, they took them to bed every night, many of them stating that "bears are not to play with but to cuddle." Of the bear owners, seven children had two, three had three, one had four, one had five, and one even had eight. Therefore, less than five percent had more than one.

Questioned about the color of their bears, ninety-two percent of the bear-owning children had normal-colored bears, being variously described as brown, fawn, ginger, yellow, tan, and gray. It was interesting to note that nearly all of the bears of other colors were owned by town children.

In reply to the question "Is there anything special or unusual about your bear?" most of the children replied in the affirmative, but it was always for purely physical reasons, i.e., because he had only one eye, ear, or leg, or because the stuffing was all about to come out. But the majority of Teddy Bears show the scars of war and age and this is the rule rather than the exception. In fact, all seem to *enjoy* ill health (or rather, the aftermath of it). Operations have become a status symbol and it is now unusual to find a bear who is still whole and in one piece.

Exactly half of the questioned children said that out of all the toys they had ever had, their Teddy Bear was their favorite. The girls answered a further question as to which they liked best, dolls or cuddly animals. Sixty-one percent preferred cuddly animals "because they are lovely and warm to take to bed and cuddle." Thirty-seven percent chose dolls because they could be dressed and undressed and they could do more with them. (This is directly opposed to what young ladies earlier in the century thought, as evinced by examples in the last chapter.) It is suspected, however, that by the phrase "could do more with them" they meant have babies and all that sort of caper, but Teddies can easily perform this function, if and when required, as you have already seen. But dolls do perform the duties of children substitutes rather more readily. Even I see that. On the other hand, one of the survey's findings was that a group of older girls had admitted that they had gone back to Teddy Bears "because I can have them sitting on my bed forever but dolls are babyish."

But in case we are overestimating children's regard for Teddy, I have to report the findings of Dr. Geiger, a professor at a New England medical center. A large group of slum children were shown a picture of a Teddy and asked to identify it. Just over forty percent thought it was a rat. Oh dear! Oh dear! What *are* things coming to?

I wonder what they'd have said if they had come face to face with the Thalidomide Teddy Bear with vestigial arms which recently came on to the French market. I am grateful to Miss Becker for this singularly unattractive bit of information. She did, however, also give me a fairly comprehensive rundown on some European Teddy Bear activities and on some of the other startling innovations in the French shops: a bear with a heart that beats, and a musical bear with a ring in his head to start off the mechanism, for examples. She also saw a chair upholstered in Teddy Bear material, the back like a bear's head and the seat forming its body. Ugh! Perhaps it's all due to the fact that "L'Ours Martin" (Martin Bear) is an unsavory character in fables of the Middle Ages in France.

Anyhow, apparently most French bears are called "Martin," though there is a TV program for the very young in which they are called (or one is) "Nounours." He tells stories of a rather high moral tone and then sails off into the air with the Sandman, looking just like a human in a bearskin. Perhaps he is, but Miss B doesn't think so. She just says how frightfully unconvincing it all is.

She was told of a French Air Force officer who slept with his Teddy Bear, and a friend's son (aged four and a half) who commiserated with his bachelor uncle because he hadn't got either a Teddy Bear to sleep with or even "une petite femme."

An Italian lady informed Miss B that Teddies had reached her country only after the last war. Her husband had given her one, but to her a bear of any sort is cold and treacherous; the usual associations of Teddies are evidently totally absent. A Spanish girl to whom Miss

157

Becker spoke knew nothing of the animal, but a Hungarian, having to limit the possessions she took out during the uprising, managed to find room for her Teddy. Austrian bears are called "Brum" bears because they growl "Brum" when they move forward. I can find no trace of Greek participation in the mystique, except for those members of the aristocracy who could afford British nannies.

There is, without doubt, a tendency among Latin races to be cold about Teddy Bears. As an example, Miss Becker cites a former French pupil of hers, sixteen years of age, who does not know or care what has become of her bear, compared with another — male, British, seventeen — who still keeps his at the end of his bed.

Rachael Feild, my British research collaborator, has a theory that Teddy Bears inspire intense interest only in countries where there aren't any real ones. Austria and Germany, she maintains, are full of the Three Bears type but not the Teddy. In Canada and wilder parts of America they don't seem half as keen on our friend as in other areas. Can it be because there they have to keep shooing the genuine article out of their fall houses?

Yet in Russia this theory doesn't seem to work. You would have thought that a country with so many ferocious bears wouldn't make toys in their image. Yet here the toy bear has flourished throughout the centuries and the Brown Bear has in fact been traditional and constant in popularity. There is naturally a strong political element in the making even of things for children, and wooden peasant and bear figures dramatize the struggle between land workers and the primitive forces of nature.

Russian nursery lore is full of Mishka the Bear, but many nineteenth-century children seem to have called him Bruin, which sort of joins the school of Dobbin (for donkey), Bunny (for rabbit), and Pussy (for guess what?). This makes the whole thing almost universal, as there is no doubt that before 1903 any toy bear in Britain and the United States was referred to as Bruin.

Yet the genuine article can only inspire fear, I'd imagine, in Russia. An animal trainer from a Soviet circus, talking on the radio recently, said that bears were the most alarming of all beasts to work with. Lions and others always look cross before they attack, but bears look at you as though you were a honeypot, whether they feel that way or not. With them the expression never changes. And that is the same with Teddies, and it's an important identification for children: it's easier, after all, to identify with a continuously benevolent expression.

But Teddies can be dangerous too! Not very long ago the British Home Office issued a warning that a few imported Polish-made Teddy Bears contained a powder which could give children penumonia. Mr. Whittle, the analyst for Bristol Corporation, became the "Teddy Bear Doctor" after this information had been received, and kept a cupboard full of the animals in his office as substitutes for the ones he had to rip apart. Well, one, as a matter of fact, for that was the sum total of Teddies found containing the fatal powder.

There is an alarming story of an almost lethal Teddy who found his way into several people's hearts. Two years ago a Mrs. Brown from Edinburgh, returning from a holiday camp, bought a large cuddly bear for her granddaughter. The wee girl loved it, played with it constantly, and slept with it in her arms at night. Then it began to deteriorate. The arms began to tear, the seams to break open, and fine powdery spray to burst from it every time it was squeezed. Because it was such a well-loved toy, it wasn't discarded but was patched and resewn. After a time the powder began appearing again. Mrs. Brown had read something in a paper about a Home Office warning and promptly relieved her granddaughter of the gift.

It turned out that this Teddy (Polish-made again) was stuffed with powdered resin which had been mixed with a small proportion of wood shavings. In the powder is a toxic chemical called formaldehyde, which is extremely harmful when either swallowed or inhaled, particularly by children. It is only fair to say that there are no more Teddies of this type on sale anywhere in Britain today, though Hong Kong imports were once believed to give off poisonous fumes in front of a fire.

The Teddy Bears
at the Circus

Publishers   THE REILLY & BRITTON CO.   Chicago

The Teddy Bears
in a Smashup

Publishers   THE REILLY & BRITTON CO   Chicago

However, "incidents" like the above resulted in a fascinating survey on the Teddy Bear World by *Which*, the magazine of the British Consumers Association. In the December 1967 issue they reported their findings:

In recent years some sinister Teddy Bears have been found with unhealthy insides that might well harm their owners in the latters' more carniverous moments. So we decided to investigate "Teddy Bears."

We have carried out post-mortems on forty, all except one of them British subjects. The odd one came from China. The bears came in all sorts of different colours, shapes, and sizes, some traditional, some less so. We set out to assess how safely they were made. We tried to test the bears in their most popular sizes, from eight and a half inches to nearly three foot tall.

Most bears had a skin of woven cotton fabric, with a pile of nylon or animal fibre. Two had woven viscous rayon, one of them with a nylon pile, the other with a viscous rayon pile. Four had animal-skin skins. All were reasonably furry.

Like us, Teddy Bears are not the same all the way through. The stuffings of the bears were kapok, man-made fibre, rag wool flock, wood wool, or pieces of foam broken up into crumbs, or a mixture of these materials. A head might be stuffed with wood-wool, arms and legs with rag flock, and the body with a mixture of the two.

It is important that these stuffings should be clean and that they should not contain any harmful substances that a child could suck out. The Rag Flock and Other Fillings Materials Regulations 1961 and 1965 lay down requirements for the cleanliness of some stuffings and there are proposals to cover most types. Most of the fillings we examined were satisfactory. . . .

Some bears had voices, usually like bleating sheep.

A bear called Sonia emitted a chime, and the Petkin Animated Teddy had a musical box in its right leg that played "Hush-a-Bye Baby." To wind it up, you had to twist its leg.

Freemans Lefray TM 1560 was more conventional, with a musical box in its body and a key sticking out of its back. One of the three samples we tested played "The Blue Danube," two played part of "The Teddy Bears' Picnic" and the three Chad Valley bears with voices had them particularly well protected in plastic casings. We did not have cuddliness tested by the real experts, but it seemed to us that the Philip Winner Giant Bear and the Shanghai Dolls Factory Bear felt rather less soft in an embrace than the others.

Arms and legs were either stitched on (the safest method of fixing them) or had moveable joints. . . . We tested the strength of the seams to see whether they were easy to pull apart in a fit of passion, or just plain curiosity. Seam strength varied quite a lot, often in one bear, but all were strong enough.

Except for the Chinese bear, which had glass eyes, all had plastic ones. Most of the bears had eyes fixed with washers. This is the safest arrangement, because if a child does pull out an eye, there are no wires sticking out on which it could hurt itself. . . .

We carried out a flammability test based on the appropriate British Standard. All except Rosebud were satisfactory; the surface of its pile burned quickly. The manufacturers tell us that Rosebud is now being made with a flameproof finish. . . .

We investigated whether the dyes were fast, because it is important that a child should not be able to suck them out. Most of the covering materials had fast dyes, but the noses of the Petkin X913 and the Petkin Animated X220 and the paws of the Pedigree 16 J/GX were not colour-fast. The body of the Pedigree 16 J/GX and the paws of the Woolworth fourteen-inch Teddy Bear were not quite colour-fast either.

There often comes a time when it is necessary to wash a Teddy Bear. Some bears are claimed to be spongeable, so we sponged them. Most of the bears that claimed to be washable were washable, but some needed careful brushing afterwards to restore their looks. The nose and mouth of Rosebud Teddy came off and the Cudlam T30 suffered some loss of appearance. Tinka-Bell Teddy Bear 493's condition could only be described as "poor" after sponging and poor Sonia chimed no more. She had started off her career with a fine chime but the current model has bells in her left ear, instead of a chime in her body.

By and large, we can give British Teddy Bears a clean bill of health. But remember that we had not tested all the T.B's that find their way into the shops around Christmas.

So concluded *Which*, and I feel rather a traitor for making the whole thing so unromantic but I feel that every side of such an important subject should be discussed. After all, it is a major industry and Colonel Henderson tells me that he has figures to prove it — namely, that one million six hundred pounds is spent every year on Teddies, who account for eighty percent of the soft toy industry. He also claims that the Teddies work hard for their living, advertising stockings, soap, tea, cereals, and coal. And I can vouch for this.

Lord Robens, the chairman of the British Coal Board, ordered twenty thousand pounds' worth of T.B.'s in a year. The symbolic figure for his organization was "Cosy," a cuddly yellow nylon bear, fourteen inches high. His name is to pinpoint solid fuel warming and he is usually shown carrying a full bucket of coal. The council also uses a live bear cub, called "Cosy" also, to take part in fuel exhibitions.

And then there is "Chad," the dapper Teddy Bear with the top hat, who is the well-known trademark of Bear Brand Limited, the American hosiery manufacturers. He started life as a grizzly bear, which was thought too unattractive for promoting feminine merchandise, though a warm undergarment worn by ladies and made by Kayser-Roth is nobly called a "teddy."

More nobly, Teddies have gone into battle on guns, tanks, and in haversacks. There is not a corner of the globe they have not penetrated. They have saved lives by intercepting bullets, breaking falls, and just being around. They've flown round the world, been drowned in floods, burned in concentration camps, and worshiped as totems. There are no cases of disloyal, treacherous, or cowardly Teddy Bears. They seem destined to survive everything, and emerge as a triumphant symbol of something or other.

The British toy-seller is convinced of their everlasting appeal. Mrs. Kathleen Lock, the chief buyer at Hamleys (London's F.A.O. Schwarz), insists that "our eternal affection for Teddies is a sure sign that the British are as sentimental as ever underneath. At least a quarter are bought by the grownups themselves. Husbands buy them for their wives when first babies arrive, boy friends buy them for fiancées, and boys and girls smuggle small substitute Teddies back to boarding school."

Yes, Mrs. Lock, I'm sure you are right, and if only I'd thought of smuggling a small Teddy back to my boarding school, I would never have lost it in the first place or indeed be writing this book.

The Creative Arts Salute Teddy

Safe were those evenings of the pre-war world
When firelight shone on green linoleum;
I heard the church bells hollowing out the sky,
Deep beyond deep, like never-ending stars,
And turned to Archibald, my safe old bear,
Whose woollen eyes looked sad or glad at me,
Whose ample forehead I could wet with tears,
Whose half-moon ears received my confidence,
Who made me laugh, who never let me down,
I used to wait for hours to see him move,
Convinced that he could breathe. One dreadful day
They hid him from me as a punishment:
Sometimes the desolation of that loss
Comes back to me and I must go upstairs
To see him in the sawdust, so to speak,
Safe and returned to his idolater.

So wrote Sir John Betjeman, the distinguished British poet who frequently gets on the non-fiction best-selling lists. The lines are an excerpt from an autobiographical book of verse entitled *Summoned by Bells* in which he pays tribute to Archibald Ormsby-Gore, his Teddy Bear companion for nearly sixty years.

"Looked sad or glad at me"—that seems a wonderful summing-up of one of Teddy's brightest virtues.

Later in the book, the poet invokes "Maud, my hateful nurse," who reacts very badly to his being late for dinner:

"You're late for dinner, John!" I feel again
That awful feeling, fear confused with thrill,

As I would be unbuttoned, bent across
Her starchy apron, screaming "Don't-Maud-Don't"
Till dissolution, bed and kindly fur
Of aged, uncomplaining Archibald.

"Mr. Archibald Ormsby-Gore has been with me as long as I can remember," says Mr. Betjeman. "He is about a foot high when he is sitting down and is very patched. His eyes are wool, his ears and nose are of some kind of cloth. Originally he was of golden fur, but this only survives on his back and behind. He is very Protestant-looking."

Recently I was privileged to meet Archibald, who had kindly asked Theodore to bring me to lunch. Now Sir John Betjeman and Mr. Ormsby-Gore have a residence in a street delightfully named Cloth Fair, which is situated in the depths of London's City district, just behind Smithfield Market. As I rounded the market, a group of burly butchers who had obviously seen me on TV, shouted: "Got your Teddy with you, mister?" "Certainly," I replied, producing my little lot from my pocket (H. H. and his American house guest were accompanying us).

The butchers swore horribly but good-humoredly. "Please desist," I admonished them. "Theodore hates swearing."

Later I discovered that Mr. Ormsby-Gore does, too. He is, in fact, far stricter about codes of behavior than most of his fellow bears. And we have had two letters from him which bear this out. The first reads:

On behalf of my Fellow Bears I wish to thank you for the mention you made of us, I understand, on the Television. Nevertheless I feel it incumbent on me to point out that no True Believer in the Triune Covenant-Keeping Jehovah can approve of a medium which indiscriminately talks to the Saved and the Damned. I hope I shall have the pleasure of meeting your own bears soon and leading them through Sovereign Grace out of Eternal Torment into the Light. Yours Faithfully, etc.

After our meeting I gathered that Mr. Ormsby-Gore had Baptist leanings and disapproved strongly of drinking and smoking. This has led to a certain amount of disagreement with Mr. Betjeman, who enjoys life to the hilt and has few aversions apart from noise and ugly modern buildings. But the two of them get along famously on the whole. They were perfect hosts to Theodore and me. A few days after our visit, Archibald enlarged on his beliefs in a letter to my bear:

> *Dear Theodore, I spend much of my time thinking of the futility of mankind and the Last Judgement, when all but us Strict and Particular Baptists will be consigned to everlasting flames. I can find scriptural warrant for all of this. I therefore give your friend, Mr. Peter Bull, permission to make the quotation he mentions, as in eternity, which I constantly contemplate, it is of no importance.*
>
> *Yours in the sure and certain hope, etc.*

This letter had a P.S.: *A Secretary is typing this, as my paws are too thick for my American-built machine.*

Baptist or Protestant, Mr. Ormsby-Gore has a tremendous personality — not very surprisingly, I suppose, — as he has to keep up with his friend Mr. Betjeman, who is one of the most beloved and revered wits in Britain. His efforts to conserve buildings of traditional heritage and his constant struggle against much of the sheer insanity of so-called progress combined with his genuine warmth have endeared him to thousands.

In the 1968 Summer Academy Exhibition in London an extraordinary picture by Jann Haworth showed him in triplicate as a Teddy Bear, his face at different angles surrounded by fur. The work was called "A Valentine to John Betjeman."

And now from a Protestant bear to an equally famous Catholic one, only this time Fictional not Factual: his name is Aloysius and he appears in Evelyn Waugh's magic novel *Brideshead Revisited*. He belongs to Lord Sebastian Flyte, the weak, exquisite hero of the book and friend of the narrator, Charles Ryder. The early setting is Oxford in the twenties, where at first Charles is disconcerted by Sebastian.

Miss Lillian Gish and one of the other stars of The Curious Savage

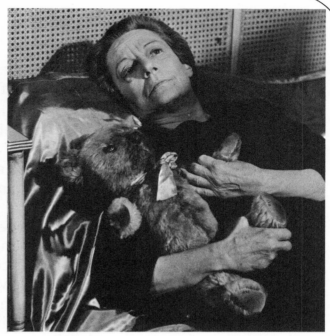

Dustin Hoffman in JOHN AND MARY *(top left),*
Tallulah Bankhead in DIE, DIE,MY DARLING
(top right), *Lana Turner and her daughter,*
Cheryl (bottom left), *Geraldine Page in*
STRANGE INTERLUDE *(bottom right),*
Sir John Betjeman (3),painting by Jann
Haworth (center left)

I knew Sebastian by sight long before I met him. That was unavoidable for, from his first week, he was the most conspicuous man of his year by reason of his beauty, which was arresting, and his eccentricities of behaviour which seemed to know no bounds. My first sight of him was in the door of Germer's and on that occasion I was struck less by his looks than by the fact that he was carrying a large teddy-bear.

"That," said the barber as I took his chair, "was Lord Sebastian Flyte. A *most* amusing young gentleman."

"Apparently," I said coldly.

"The Marquis of Marchmain's second boy. His brother, the Earl of Brideshead, went down last term. Now he was *very* different, quite like an old man. What do you suppose Lord Sebastian wanted? A hair-brush for his teddy-bear; it was to have very stiff bristle, *not*, Lord Sebastian said, to brush him with, but to threaten him with a spanking when he was sulky. He bought a very nice one with an ivory back and he's having 'Aloysius' engraved on it—that's the bear's name."

The students become great friends but they don't leave Aloysius behind, as when one day they go for a drive in an open-seater Morris Cowley.

Sebastian's teddy-bear sat at the wheel. We put him between us—"Take care he's not sick," and drove off.

At one point in the novel Charles gets a letter from Sebastian in which he says: "I have a good mind not to take Aloysius to Venice. I don't want him to meet a lot of horrid Italian bears and pick up bad habits."

Later, in a discussion about religion, Charles the skeptic challenges Sebastian's beliefs:

"Do you think you can kneel down in front of a statue and say a few words, not even out loud, just in your mind, and change the weather? Or that some saints are more influential than others, and you must get hold of the right one to help you on the right problem?"

"Oh yes," says Sebastian. "Don't you remember last term when I took Aloysius and left him behind I didn't know where. I prayed like mad to St. Anthony of Padua that morning, and immediately after lunch there was Mr. Nichols at Canterbury Gate with Aloysius in his arms, saying I'd left him in a cab."

Americans, too, have written about Teddies, though not, perhaps, so lyrically. One writer of verse, whose name seems to have passed almost into oblivion, has, with the exception of A. A. Milne, probably contributed more to Teddy's reputation than any other writer. He had two names, as a matter of fact: the main one was Seymour Eaton; the other, Paul Piper, he always put in brackets.

He created two bears called "The Roosevelt Bears," and the four volumes in which they appeared between 1906 and 1910 enjoyed a tremendous vogue. They dealt with two characters, "Teddy G" (Good) and "Teddy B" (Bad), whose travels and adventures were richly illustrated by Floyd Campbell. Such was the success of the books that the drawings with captions spread to postcards, notepaper, and even pottery and glass. The appeal that they had for the American public seems to have prefigured the enormous success of Milne and his illustrator, Ernest Shephard, twenty years later.

In a preface to the second volume, Seymour Eaton wrote:

When in the autumn of 1905 I created the characters of Teddy B. and Teddy G., I builded better than I knew. I brought these bears out of their mountain den in Colorado and started them on their tour of the East to teach children that animals, even bears, may have some measure of human feeling; that the primary purpose of animals is not necessarily that of supplying sport for the hunter. That this lesson has been abundantly taught is proven by the over-

MORE ABOUT

Teddy B. and Teddy G.

THE

ROOSEVELT BEARS

Being
Volume Two

Depicting their further
Travels and Adventures.

By

Seymour Eaton

(PAUL PIPER)

Illustrated by
R.K. Culver

EDWARD STERN & COMPANY, Inc
PHILADELPHIA
MCMVII

whelming welcome given the Teddy Bears by the boys and girls of the United States; and it is safe to say that the traditional "bear will get you" has now and forever lost its frightening significance. The book is a sequel to *The Travels and Adventures of the Roosevelt Bears*, and completes the story of Teddy B. and Teddy G. from Colorado to Washington. The third volume will report in jingle and picture the tour of the Teddy Bears abroad.

And indeed it did:

> *As they left for London at noon that day*
> *They thanked the king for the royal way*
> *He had entertained; and this said they,*
> *"If you'll visit us in the U.S.A.,*
> *When we get back to our home again*
> *And stop with us in our mountain den,*
> *We'll give you food and naught to do,*
> *And let you sleep all winter through*
> *And dream of castles and suck your paw,*
> *It beats all the kingdoms you ever saw."*
> *The king just laughed as the train pulled out,*
> *But he said to himself as he turned about,*
> *"It would help me carry my country's cares*
> *If every home had Teddy Bears."*

As will be observed from the reproduction of one of the drawings, the bears are both far more human *and* ursine than the usual Teddy and yet they have tremendous natural character. It is very curious indeed that the books have vanished from circulation and are so difficult to get hold of.

The Teddy seems to have taken far longer to establish himself in British literature. A book published around 1910 called *The Cockyolly Bird*, by Mabel Dearmer, had a certain amount of success and was turned into a popular children's play of the same name. It featured "Little Edward," who in the stage production did a Sandman's dance *and* a Tango. In a letter describing her memories of him, a Mrs. Fowler brilliantly evokes the whole Edwardian period.

> *Little Edward drops out of the story quite early, as he wants to remain at the North Pole to try and become a real bear. The Polar Bear, his friend, who admires him tremendously, tries to become a Teddy Bear. They neither of them succeed and Little Edward has to go back to his nursery, a sunlit nursery with tulips in the windowboxes, and a little boy called Kit with two cross nurses and a nursery maid all to himself. There is a beautiful mother who floats round with a rose in her belt, who sometimes summons her child to her dressing room to look at him or give him a present. His adoration of this lovely lady is understandable, as all the scolding was done by his two cross nurses.*

"You can imagine the incredulous delight of a modern mother on reading this, in the intervals of sloshing away at the sink," comments Mrs. Fowler dryly.

Yes, Teddies, literally speaking, seem to have taken a bit of time to really get going in Britain, but for the last fifty years they have held a very firm grip on the affections of the reading public. Indeed, for the last forty we've had Rupert, a highly individual bear who always wears a red jersey, check trousers, a muffler round his neck, and heavy boots on his feet.

A lady called Mary Tourtel created the story of Rupert, and on November 8, 1920, "The Adventures of a Little Lost Bear" began with captions in verse by Miss T's husband, a sub-editor on the *Express*. The feature became so popular that a Rupert League was started, but apparently it had become so unwieldy by 1935 because of its great success that it was brought to an end. In the same year Miss Tourtel's sight failed and she had to resign. An attempt to do a photographic story job on Rupert flopped; finally, A. E. Bestall was called in to become the Rupert artist and for the last thirty-odd years his drawings have

177

appeared daily in the newspaper, with only two breaks. Once Rupert was crowded out by a Churchill wartime speech and once by the death of Pope John. A "Rupert Annual" is published every year.

It would be impossible to list *all* the books in which Teddy Bears are mentioned, and frightfully boring if I did. However, I would have you know that almost every writer of distinction appears to be fully conscious of their importance. From Jean Genet (in *Our Lady of the Flowers*) via Aldous Huxley (in *The Giaconda Smile*) to Violet Weingarten (in *Guide to Traveling with Children in Europe*) to Ian Fleming (in *Casino Royale*), it seems that literature can hardly survive without reference to the dear little creatures. But I would like to pay more than lip service to tomes in which Teddy plays an active part.

In Henri de Motherlant's *Les Jeunes Filles* I seem to remember that both Mlles. Dandillot and Costals take one to bed with them —quite apart from each other.

In *Ask Agamemnon*, by Jenni Hall (author of *The Ha-Ha*), a pitch-black Teddy Bear gets mixed up in a ritual killing with baffling mythological connotations.

Books about Teddies for children are of course legion. The majority are for the younger reader or even non-reader and therefore profusely illustrated. One of the better-known series is *Big Teddy and Little Teddy*, written by Mrs. J. C. Cradock and drawn by Honor G. Appleton, which deals with Big Teddy, who is always in trouble, and Little Teddy, who is rather macabrely one-armed *and* one-legged. Mrs. Cradock also wrote profusely about *Pamela's Teddy Bears*, all of whom are constructed normally *as far as I know*.

The Shoe-Shop Bears, Bears Back in Business and *Hannibal and the Bears* are three delightful books by Margaret Baker, classified, somehow, as "educational." Two of the titles are self-explanatory, but the one about Hannibal shows how three Teddy Bears rescue discarded animals from the town rubbish dump and find Hannibal, an elephant, there.

There were eight little books published by the Reilly and Britton Company in Chicago in 1907, with titles like *The Teddy Bears in a Smash-Up* and *The Teddy Bears in Hot Water*. The small boy who has charge of the bears in this series is rather alarming-looking, so it's no surprise that they all land in a good deal of trouble.

In a series of primers for reading in first to third grades in American schools Dick, Jane, and Sally are the main humans in the stories, but a character called Tim the Teddy Bear features strongly.

Several strip-type cartoons have Teddies in them. One popular with children was called *Buster Brown and His Dog Tighe* and Pogo the Invincible quite often runs across Barnstable Bear during his adventures.

In Britain, quite apart from Rupert, there are many steadily popular characters, like Paddington (a bear called after the Station). On television we have Sooty and Andy Pandy to keep the viewers Teddy-conscious.

A few books for the sophisticated adolescent have appeared from time to time. A good recent example was *The Teddy Bear Habit*, by James Lincoln Collier. In it a young fellow called George Stable always has a Teddy Bear beside him for moral support, as he constantly feels failure and impending doom. He loses the Spelling Bee because he doesn't have the animal around. But when he makes a speech at the school assembly, he triumphs because he has set the bear offstage where he can see him.

"If you think a book about a Teddy Bear and a kid in Greenwich Village is apt to be silly," wrote a tuned-in reviewer, "you've got another think coming."

The Teddies of the theatre are not always so endearing and clear-cut. Often they appear as symbols or alter egos. In *Look Back in Anger*, John Osborne used bears as a kind of desperate therapy, for his two warring protagonists every now and then lose themselves in the morass of a fantasy of bears and squirrels.

It was the "one way of escaping from everything," says poor tor-

179

Some toys hate war.

Some toys are furry. And they are for holding and hugging in your bed.

And some toys are pully. They are for pulling behind you on a string.

And some toys you can swing from. (If you can get daddy to hang them up.)

And some toys are made by people in Appalachia. And they tell you something about the world and how people are with each other.

But no toys teach you how to hate or kill.

Not at Georg Jensen they don't.

GEORG JENSEN 53rd and Fifth, New York City
Scarsdale Manhasset Millburn Ridgewood / Paramus

Goldilocks and the ~~3~~ 45 bears

tured Alison to her friend, "a sort of unholy priesthood of being animals to one another. We could become little furry creatures with little furry brains. Full of dumb uncomplicated affection for each other. Playful careless creatures in their cozy zoo for two. A silly symphony for people who couldn't bear the pain of being human beings any longer. And now, even they are dead, poor little silly animals. They were all love and no brains." And with that she puts the bear and the squirrel back in the chest of drawers.

Sometimes Teddy is used in a sinister and alarming way, as in Richard Fleischer's powerful film *Compulsion*, which told the story of Leopold and Loeb (in the film they are called Judd and Artie), two college students who, in the twenties, murdered a comrade for the mere sheer thrill of it. In an early scene, Artie castigates Judd for losing his spectacles, possibly at the scene of the murder. He sits sprawled on a chair "with a stuffed teddy bear propped on his lap."

> JUDD: The last time I wore them — I was studying — in that old tweed jacket.
>
> ARTIE: The same one he had on yesterday — the same one he tossed on the ground when he got that brilliant idea about hiding the body. He left them there like a calling-card, didn't he, Teddy?
>
> (*He slips his hand behind the teddy bear's head and chuckles gleefully as Teddy nods agreement*)
>
> JUDD: No, I didn't drop them! You picked up my coat and tossed it to me! That's when they fell out. I agree it was inexcusable to have them in my pocket but I didn't drop them.
>
> (*Artie smiles gently and transfers his attention back to Teddy, resuming his dreamy, childlike and increasingly irritating monologue*)
>
> ARTIE: He agrees with us, Teddy . . . isn't that lovely? (*Teddy nods*) He agrees it was all our fault . . . We said dump the body in the lake, but no, he said . . . nobody will ever find him there . . . not in a million years he said.

JUDD: Will you stop that?

ARTIE: Shut up! We're not talking to you. The first guy by on his way to work pulled him out of that stinking pipe? (*Resuming with Teddy*) Why do you suppose he picked the pipe, Teddy? . . . Look at him! (*Teddy's head whips round*) Because it was the first place handy? (*Teddy nods*) Mmmmmmmm. I think you're right, and you know what else I think? (*Teddy's head swings round curiously*) I think he never wanted to go through with it, anyway.

JUDD: That's not true and you know it, Artie! We both agreed it would be the true test of the superior intellect and I . . .

ARTIE (*Whooping*): Superior intellect! What do you think of that, Teddy? You and I work out a perfect, beautiful crime, then this superior intellect tries to see how many ways he can find to . . .

(*He breaks off as there is a rap at the door. It is Max, a slightly suspicious fellow student, and after a short scene he starts to leave but suddenly notices Teddy*)

MAX: What's that for? Protection?

ARTIE: Teddy? Oh, I always take him everywhere. He's indispensable.

(*With a quick twist he snaps the teddy bear's head from his body. A flask is revealed inside*)

A slightly more sympathetic role was enacted by a bear in a play by John Patrick called *The Curious Savage* (produced in New York in October, 1950). This bear belonged to a Mrs. Savage, an eccentric lady, played by Miss Lillian Gish, who lived in a sort of home for bizarre old girls. On Teddy's first appearance (the stage directions say "he is somewhat the worse for wear") one of the other ladies (Fairy), on first catching sight of him, thinks he's alive.

She asks anxiously: "It won't bite?" and Mrs. Savage replies: "It won't shed, lay eggs or bark. And to the best of my knowledge it's

183

unvexed by sex. It couldn't be less trouble." Fairy is relieved, and charmingly says: "In any case, any friend of yours is a friend of mine."

One of the other inmates, who stopped talking some twenty years previously, takes a great fancy to the bear, which Mrs. Savage carries everywhere with her. Mrs. S is terribly worried about getting a new eye for him. Though she is a very rich woman, she has been put in the home by her unscrupulous relatives. She has converted all her money into bonds, which she has hidden. The family is being driven slowly mad: where oh where has she hidden those bonds? She has, of course, hidden them in Teddy's head. She eventually reveals the truth and everything turns out all right for almost everybody. The last stage direction of the play reads: "Only the Teddy Bear, sitting alone in a spot of light in the surrounding darkness, is seen as THE CURTAIN FALLS."

Possibly the most important part ever played by a Teddy Bear in the theatre was in *One Fair Daughter*, by Jean Scott Rogers, produced in London just after World War II. In it a bear was the later ego of the young, beautiful, but impossible Gina, played by Diane Cilento, whose egocentricity drove an elderly woman and, finally, herself to suicide.

Remarkably, the character of Gina was based on a real girl who, in fact, never saw the play but did commit suicide some years later. She had been passionately devoted to a Teddy Bear who was cremated with her.

In a very dramatic scene at the end, the bereaved young husband finally gets hold of the animal, for which he's been searching for three weeks.

"He's all that I have left of her and sometimes I think Wuzzie was the only thing Gina ever loved. I shall keep him always to remember her by."

His friend tries to remonstrate, but he goes on: "You don't understand. Wuzzie was part of Gina, a sort of double identity. Had been since she was a little girl. It used to irritate me at times, but she would have grown out of it once we had had a child of our own."

As you can see, Teddy finds his way to the boards and silver screen quite a lot. I'd like to draw your attention to yet some other notable appearances. He was in *Alfie* (remember the abortion scene?), *Cabaret* (Sally Bowles throws him on the bed when she arrives to set up house with the American author), and most recently in a sensational French play called *Les Yeux Créves* by Jean Caul, in which Alain Delon was his owner, though he lent him to Mme. Marie Bell while they were both high on cocaine.

As far as I know, no Teddy Bear has been knighted for his services to the theatre but he certainly has a place there. Over the years I've had some interesting communications from bear actors. One, whose spelling leaves a good deal to be desired, tells me that his mistress does a lot of plays during which he gets put in "the most kepuliar places under the sofa, or in a coal scuttle or up a 'chemney.'"

Another, obviously more sophisticated Thespian told me that his greatest success was as the dead Astynax in a production of *The Trojan Women*, though his performance in *Five Finger Exercise* had been "well thought of by many." His name was Growler. He evidently doesn't seem to have thought the game worth the candle, for he retired from the theater after a couple of setbacks. He now lives on the Cornish coast, where he and another old bear busker called Waffle swap endless stories of their theatrical triumphs.

From the theatrical world to the world of song publishing: Between 1907 and 1911 over forty titles beginning with the words "Teddy" or "Teddy Bear" were registered for copyright. So heaven knows how many songs there were, depicting the activities of the dear things.

A lady called Elsie Phelan had them "Going Walking," "At Their Noonday Rest," "Playing Leapfrog," "Returning Home," and just plain "Waltzing," whereas Mr. (or Mrs.) O'Grady had them "At Home," "Coming from School," "Going to School," and even "*In* School," briefly I hope, in order to take part in "Playing Football," "At the Dance," and "Coming From the Dance," "In Slumberland," and, strangest of all, "In an Airship."

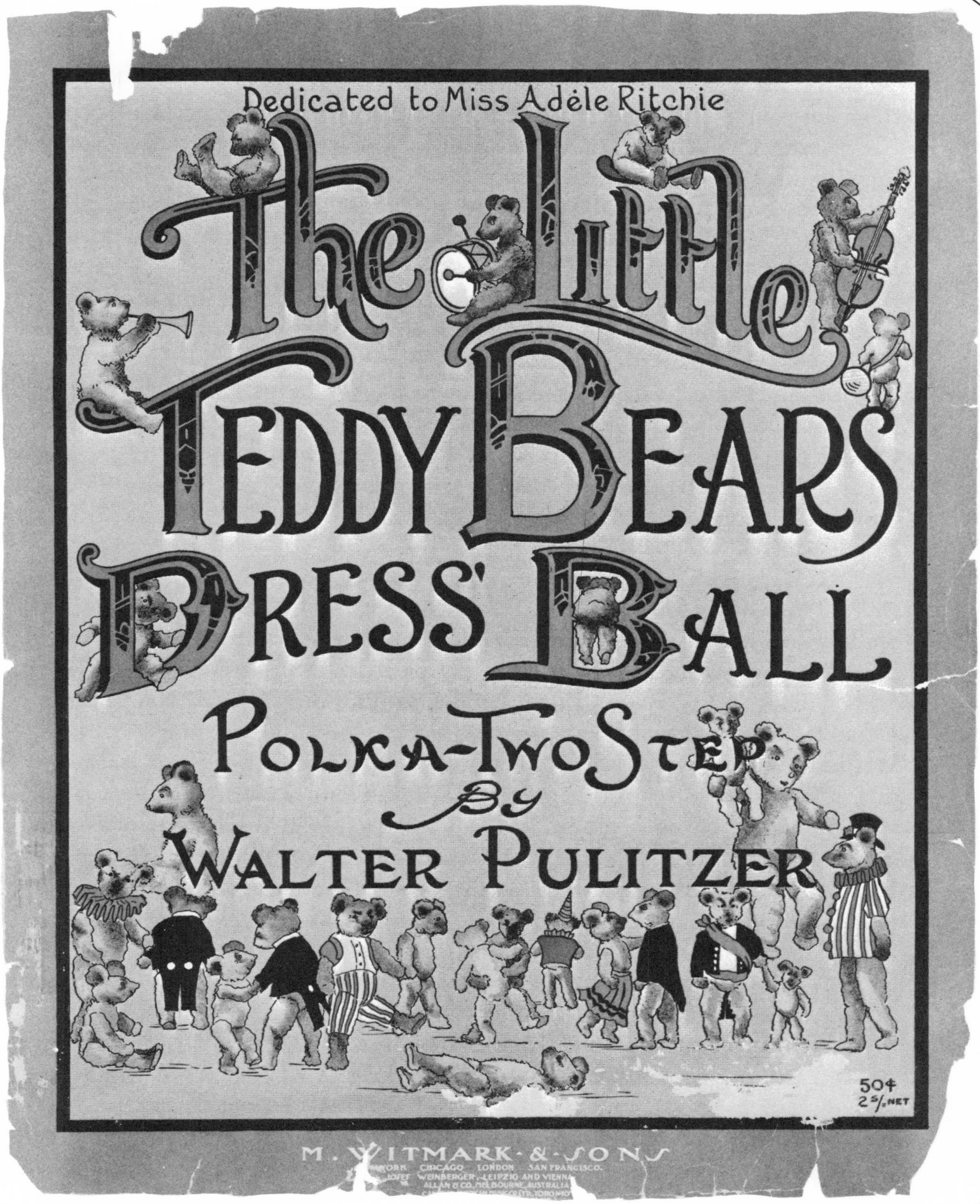
Dedicated to Miss Adèle Ritchie
The Little
Teddy Bears
Dress' Ball
Polka-Two Step
By
Walter Pulitzer
50¢
2s/. NET
M. Witmark & Sons
York Chicago London San Francisco.
Weinberger, Leipzig and Vienna
Allan & Co. Melbourne, Australia

There was a Teddy Bear March and a Teddy Trombone March, to say nothing of a Teddy Bear Rag and a simple Teddy Bear Song. There was a Teddy Bears' Dance and a Dance of the Teddy Bears, not to be confused with "The Little Teddy Bears' Dress Ball." Numerous titles just had the word "Teddy Bear" or "Teddy," and the similarity of all the songs on this theme was quite extraordinary during this period. Music shops must have got exasperated by their customers' getting their requirements even slightly wrong. For instance, should they have asked for a song about "Teddy and Home" they would have been faced with the following alternatives: "Teddy's Coming Home," "Teddy's Come Home," "Teddy's Coming Home Again," and the peremptory "Teddy Come Home" and "Teddy Come Back." "Teddy, We're Glad You're Here" was obviously written to celebrate the traveler's return from such outposts as the jungle, where he habitually adjourned (to judge from "Teddy in the Jungle" and "Teddy the Jungle Bogie-Man").

In Britain the Teddies are very athletic indeed in the song-title field. They boogie, they dance, they frolic, they do the cakewalk, they walk quite simply, they touch the ground, they get mixed up with hobby-horses, they march, and, of course, Have a Picnic.

"The Teddy Bear's Picnic" has had, you may be amazed to hear, a most checkered career as a song. It was originally brought out by Witmark's in New York to coincide with Roosevelt's bid for re-election in 1907. It was later published by Feldman's in London. Light orchestras played it quite a lot at first, but it was soon relegated to use as circus background music. In 1930 Bert Feldman approached Jimmy Kennedy to write new lyrics to the song. Kennedy, later to become world-famous as the author of "The Isle of Capri" and other big hits, was at that time a struggling writer and went home to reset the "T.B.'s Picnic" in his bed-sitting-room. It was then used by a kiddies' troupe in a Manchester pantomime. Still, nothing really startling happened to the song until Henry Hall, the head of the BBC musical department, started looking for children's items. His manager got hold of the song;

it was immediately re-orchestrated and put on the air by a well-known singer of the period, Val Rosing. The response was electrifying: the BBC was swamped with requests, and Henry Hall and his own orchestra rushed out a recording which has been a best seller for over thirty years and is now in its third million.

Probably the next two Teddy Bear songs in order of popularity are "Me and My Teddy Bear," written by a Mr. Coots, and "Teddy Bear," sung by a Mr. Elvis Presley, who, after recording the piece, was sent about eight million, three hundred thousand and forty-four T. Bears by adoring fans.

But of course it was with Theodore Roosevelt that so many of the earlier American compositions were linked. There was, for instance, a Teddy Roosevelt march and a two-step, and a song with a curious lyric, admonishing the President of the United States:

> *Our President's a naughty man.*
> *He's bold and bad I know.*
> *He shoots poor little Teddy Bears*
> *My Nursey told me so.*
> *I'm going to write to Washington*
> *If you don't think I'll dare*
> *I'll show you, for he cannot shoot*
> *My Teddy Teddy Bear.*

It's actually "Nursey" who should be shot for passing on such wildly inaccurate information. The one thing the President was renowned for in this connection was *not* shooting little bears.

Then there was a jaunty electioneering song to spur him on. It was called "Teddy, You're a Bear," and was written by Ring Lardner.

> *Teddy, you are a bear, we want you where*
> *Our one best bet should be.*
> *Teddy, pack your grip, get ready to take a trip*
> *To Washington D.C.*
> *You'll make 'em treat us right, you're not too proud to fight,*
> *You'll see that we prepare,*

We're tired of being goats, we'll give you all our votes,
For Teddy, you're a bear.
Teddy, last time you ran we didn't dream, old man,
There'd be so much to do:
We thought the job a snap, too small a job, old chap,
For a man like you.
Now we know otherwise, now we apologize,
Forgive us, Teddy dear,
Get out the old stick, swing it and swing it quick,
We're with you this year.

You'll be sorry to hear that I have so far been unable to trace the words of a song called "I've Got a Pain in My Sawdust," which, I gather, was greatly in vogue in the twenties and was apt to be sung in public (or private) by any child dressed as a Teddy Bear.

In the earlier part of the century there were many revue numbers with a Teddy Bear motif. Teddie Gerrard, a popular British star of the period, was constantly making merry with them. One of her songs, from a revue called *Bric-a-Brac*, produced in London in 1915, was all the rage:

Everybody calls me Teddy,
T. E. Double D. Y.
Yankee-Swankee
Full of Hanky-Panky
With the R.S.V.P. Eye
All day long they telephone
Keep repeating hard,
Are you there,
Little Teddy Bear?
Naughty Naughty One Gerrard.

Gerrard, by the way, was also once the name of a London telephone exchange. From Pelissier's Follies in 1909 had come this delightful number:

I wish I had a Teddy Bear
To sit upon my knee.
I'd take him with me everywhere,
To cuddle up with me.
I'd scorn young men,
No lover then
My lot in life should share,
They all might go to Jericho
If I'd a Teddy Bear.

Come on, all together now! "I Wish I Had a Teddy Bear . . ."

191

Themselves

Me and my Teddy Bear
Have no worries,
Have no care!
Me and my Teddy Bear
Just play and play all day.
I love my Teddy Bear,
He's got one eye and got no hair,
But I love my Teddy Bear,
We play and play all day!
Every night he's with me
When I climb up the stairs,
And by my bed he listens
   until I say my prayers!
Oh! Me and my Teddy Bear
Have no worries,
Have no care!
Me and my Teddy Bear
Just play and play all day.

It is only right and proper that I should give over this last chapter to the Bears Themselves. They are just as articulate as Other Persons. A small percentage of my correspondence has come directly from them, and though it is possible that they've sometimes had to seek outside help for technically getting their views across, there is no doubt whatsoever that these views come from the brains they have been given.

I've got to know some of my befurred Pen Pals quite well and they've become very real to me. Mark you (as my mother used to say), our relationships have had their ups and downs. Like so many minority groups these days, the Teddies are impatient to get things going in their direction. Although they realize that this book cannot fail to enhance their already not inconsiderable reputation, they are intolerant of any delays in its publication. Some even opine that they may have passed on by the time it finally comes out.

Another slight cloud in our association is that most of them are very publicity-conscious. I find that I have only to speak on the radio or TV about Teddy Bears for the letter-box to be jammed with querulous letters. "Why didn't you mention *me*?" is the recurring complaint, and I've had to give up bringing in the names of particular friends of mine, for fear of inciting jealousy and discontent among the ranks. But they are, one and all, desperately keen to help. And some of the information I've received is extremely valuable.

For instance, Mr. Edward Bear paints a vivid picture of life in a normal British household as seen through his eyes:

11 New Street
Wells, Somerset
May 12th, 1966

Dear Sir,

Your letter in last week's Spectator *has come to my notice, and as a bear aged forty-eight, whose authority in a family has increased over the years, I am sending you some observations from my experience.*

I joined the family soon after the end of the '14-'18 war as a companion to a little girl of two. When she was five she decided to make me growl fortissimo; she jumped on my growler cords, which suffered irreparable damage and it was only about ten years ago that medical science supplied me with a grafted growl (of higher pitch, but I accepted it). Soon after the loss of my growl, too active participation at a party caused my head to come off, and while awaiting transport to the hospital I had the most undignified experience of my life. The girl's parents, their bridge guests, and two maids of the household played, in

194

*the hall late at night, a round game called "Broken Bottles"
with my head. Never since have I suffered such lack of
respect.*

*It was, however, when the girl grew up and married
that I really became an Elder Statesman. The girl's father
had died, so the new young family lived on in our childhood
home, and twin boys were born in 1946. One twin soon
acquired a Bear of character called Teddah, and the
younger twin a sheepskin little Teddy and a small grey
bunny named Harris Rabbit, who claims to be of Anglo-
Chinese extraction and is a witty person much given to the
consumption of alcohol. Seven years ago a baby bear was
knitted for a friend's child, but, when he was ready to be
packed up, we all, boys and parents too, felt we could not
let him go to be at the mercy of a small girl. So Ted the
Bear stayed on, and I have brought him up and am his
Guardian and Tutor.*

*My influence is paramount in the family now. My
advice is sought on many matters and I am indisputably in
charge of the small folk.*

*With all good wishes to one who must have an intelli-
gent appreciation of Teddy Bears.*

> *I am, sir,*
> *Yours very truly*
> *Edward Bear* (signed)

The next letter was written on May 27, 1966.

Dear Sir,

*I accept your compliments with pleasure and extend
mine to you. I am happy to enlarge on the life of our little
community.*

*First, our domestic celebrations: the entire house-
hold assembles when Christmas, Easter, and birthday presents are distributed. We ourselves do not celebrate our
birthdays, some of which are unknown, but we all receive*

Teddy Batt

Teddy Sales.

Ally Belby.

M Turnbull

French Teddy

The bears of the second grade

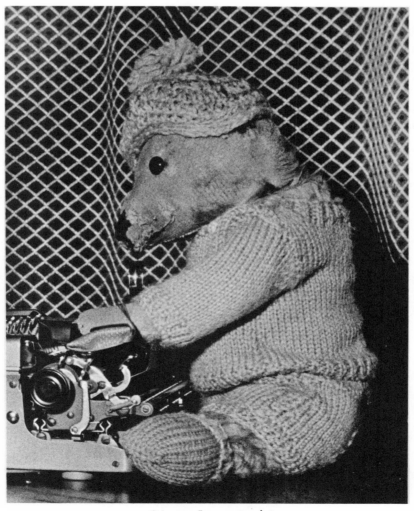

Miss Sally

Theodore Bear invites you to a tea party
at Brown's Hotel in Dover Street. W.1 on
Monday October 13th 4-5.30 p.m to celebrate
publication of Peter Bull's book "BEAR WITH
ME".

TEA
HUNNY

R.S.V.P.
149 King's Road
S.W.3.

Ginger Jones, typist

Christmas and Easter presents, and give some. We are present at all purely family celebrations and all have a taste of any drinks going. Except for a few close friends of the family we are rather snobbish about mixing. So many people have stupid conversations and are so uncivilised that we do not grant audiences indiscriminately. Recently, a Person called while Ted and I were downstairs (having had our honey). Ted had been wearing a handsome silver medal on a ribbon round his neck and the Person suddenly poked it fiercely into his chest, saying: "That shouldn't be there — it's valuable!"

For a moment we feared Ted was about to strike her. He took a deep breath and clenched his fists, but my training bore fruit and he held his peace. My owner said firmly: "It's in very good hands," and Ted continues to wear his medal.

Politically we are all very Right Wing. Certainly we are charitable and have no wish to Grind the Faces of the Poor but I know where to draw the line and I expect it to be toed.

I cannot lay down any clear rules about our wearing of clothes. I used not to wear any, but I have taken to them as I grow older, partly for warmth and partly for vanity, but largely because my skin or fur is now showing signs of age. Most of our clothes, as you'd expect, are hand-made.

Be so kind as to let me know if I can be of any further assistance to you; I shall be indeed interested in the ultimate results of your researches.

With sentiments distingués from us all,

I am, yours very truly, Edward Bear

Some of my ursine correspondents just want to tell me about the extraordinary things that have happened to them. One was shipwrecked and had to spend several anxious hours in a lifeboat before being rescued and taken to Cape Town, where he "had another unpleasant experience, being severely mauled by a dog."

Water seems to offer a frequent hazard for bears. A number of them have fallen into lakes, rivers, and seas. Sixty-five-year-old Teddy Rogers had a close call in Lake George when his owner fell overboard from a steamer. No wonder he admits to being in pretty bad shape!

It is curious how human old bears become when they talk about retiring. "Old Ted Lewin," who is well on in his fifties, packed it all in a few years ago. His last job was to play with his original owner's two grandsons. Then: "Everyone advised me to give up, and rather than have a sudden collapse I thought it best to take their advice." He now lives in a quiet little English fishing port.

Old Ted had one or two exciting experiences in the last war, and during the London blitzes, had a remarkable escape. He and his owner were staying at a lodging house on the outskirts of London when a fire bomb hit the roof. Luckily the head of the family was on leave and able to help them escape.

"Everyone but me was in the cellar," wrote Old Ted, "and as the flames got nearer I was very thankful to see Master in the doorway. He snatched me and Mistress's lipstick up (he told me afterwards in confidence that he thought we were the two things she would most want to have by her in an emergency like this). Then, taking her by the hand, he got us both into the street to look for a public shelter. When we went to look next morning the house was a shell and only the walls were standing. I still have all my factualities," he ends.

Except, I imagine, spelling.

It's only natural for a bear to feel his age and want to have a nice long lie-down after years of faithful and loyal service. A sixty-year-old Somerset bear I know has a cub to run errands for him now when his feet hurt. The two of them visit hospitals to help the boys and girls get well; the senior bear relates a never-ending story about how once upon a time he caught a fish while out on a boat in Ireland. In those days Ted lived in a Regency house in his birthplace of Weston-Super-Mare, a super name for a seaside resort, and all he thinks about now is returning there.

199

It is mainly the older generation of Teddy Bears who write to me of their experiences. What a vivid memory they have of their youth. One goes so far as to remember his christening. And so he should, considering that he had his name tattooed on the bottom of his paws. "Teddy" was inscribed with marking-ink on the left one and "Holland," the name of the family he had adopted, on his right. "I am pleased to say that I have never felt any ill effect from the tattooing though the words have worn very faint."

He had a long spell wrapped in newspaper in the depths of a linen basket. Then one day his mistress took him out, gave him a thorough checkup (for moths, etc.), pronounced him fit, and sat him down in an easy chair in her bedroom, where he reports he is still very happy.

Many bears don't mind admitting that they are rather long in the tooth, to say nothing of their receding hairline, and Mister Bear, who has spent most of his life with Miss Marrian of London, is brutally frank about his own appearance. But then he has been through a lot. Listen:

I came to London from Canada in 1904 to befriend a baby called Pauline Marrian, who was born just then. Ours was a nannie-ruled nursery, so I know all about washing my paws before meals and the awful warning, when things are being specially jolly and hilarious, that "there'll be tears before bedtime."

I was handsome when young. About eighteen inches tall with light brown fur and a growly voice. But I lost my looks early. Those odd Turkish baths (beginning in the oven and ending on the clothes line) which were prescribed after measles and whooping cough and such, though very enjoyable, rather took the stuffing out of me. This led to several operations, which left scars, so I took to wearing clothes, very much against my will. However when the war came—the second one in 1939—Pauline got me a siren suit. I didn't mind wearing that because, after all, Mr. Churchill wore one, didn't he? I am not quite bald and one eye is larger than the other because I unfortunately mislaid an eye and a much bigger bear, who didn't need his any more, kindly passed one on to me.

In 1925, Pauline and I gave a twenty-first birthday party for the Teddy Bears we knew in our nursery days. Some of them came all alone by post. I believe they boasted for years about this hazardous journey, whereas I used often to go and stay with friends in Cornwall and always found the post a most comfortable and convenient means of travel. I thought *nothing* of it.

In 1937 Pauline and I went to live in Hungary, and there I met the nicest Teddy Bear I've ever known. When his friends Tamas and Balint had to go into hospital, he came to stay with me and taught me Hungarian. In return I taught him English and we wrote to the boys every week in each other's language to show them how we were getting on. This bear was lost in the siege of Budapest.

During the Second World War, Pauline and I were on an ack-ack gunsite at Wormwood Scrubbs. The chaps gave me a tin hat (well, it was cardboard really) and I secretly hoped to become an N.C.O. in due course, or even an officer, but life is full of disappointments, as Nannie used to say, and soldiering isn't really my line.

I expect you know Miss Carrell Bear, who never missed a performance during the run of Clemence Dane's play *Eighty in the Shade* at the Globe Theatre? I wrote her a fan letter suggesting she should change her agent, for she hadn't even got her name on the programme, though she should of course have been starred. Both she and Dame Sybil Thorndike, who *did* star in the piece, replied most kindly and I should like to know what Carrell Bear's commitments are now.

I hope this letter is all right because to some newspaper reporter you said "No Actual Bears, thank you," which may mean that you only want to hear about us and not from us. Well, I haven't a secretary and Pauline is much too busy to write for me, so I thought I'd do it myself. You can easily put my letter in the wastepaper basket if you don't want it.

Mister Bear needn't have worried. But not all the ursine correspondents are so modest. Bears Unlimited wrote in to say that "we Steiff Bears in Cambridge, Massachusetts, have a fine well-established concern here, with nine bears currently vacationing at our country place, while we look after things here in town."

Another bear, who used to live with the late Peter Swanwick, the English actor, sent me a lovely photograph of himself looking out a window. It had a rather laconic biography on the back: "Pooh Edward Bear born Christmas 1939 to Miss Gillian Ashby. Fond of travel. Loves holidays in North Wales. Watched Mulberry Harbour being built. Largest of a family of thirteen. An acting bear who has toured. Favourite music: the end of Beethoven's Violin Concerto."

But I'm afraid several of my correspondents tend to be of a sentimental turn of mind. A lot of them see themselves in relation to their owners in the roles of husband, wife, lover, or housekeeper — or all of these! "Mum goes to business and I stay at home to look after things and be there to greet her when she gets back." That's one recurring theme. Others consider themselves in an advisory capacity — far more sensible of them, if you ask me. ("If she has a problem, it seems that she likes to talk it out with me.")

But many are just plain uninhibited and live lives of splendid egotistical eccentricity. Take Sir Gangy de Brownman, for example, who sends me regular bulletins. He has been decorated with the "Scarlet Order of Wrexhall" for "service in the field." When I politely asked him what field, he replied: "Plowed of course, silly." His wardrobe includes a full admiral's uniform, Regency rig for *bals masqués*, a

Sir Gangy de Brownman, with Algy in center

hacking jacket, and a silk suit in case he's asked to lunch at Buckingham Palace. What do I mean "in case"? It's for *when* he's asked to "Buck House," as he calls it. He is a First Baronet, with New York Wall Street Casuals (whatever *they* are) and a great friend in the person of Algy, a two-foot-high rabbit!

Algy, who just happens to be one of the most famous animals in the world, recently took up the whole of the front page of the color supplement of *The Observer*. But Sir Gangy managed to get his features in, as well, on Algy's passport photograph, taken especially so that the rabbit could accompany Sir Alec Rose on his historic voyage across the world and back in *Lively Lady*.

Sir Gangy kept Algy *au fait* with the news by sending him tapes and letters. Is it surprising to learn that both of them are contemplating their autobiographies?

Theodore, my small friend, has his own Pen Pals. One is a rag doll called Honey, whose mistress sings to her to lull her to sleep.

"Does your master read or sing to *you*?" she asked Theodore.

He replied: "No, thank God!"

One of his regular correspondents is a Miss Ophelia Bear, whose owner is having emotional problems. She is in love with a doctor older than herself who won't marry her because he thinks he's too old.

"Paula is very unhappy," reports Ophelia Bear, "and sometimes I get all wet from her holding me real close and crying. I don't think that difference in age is all that important, do you?"

"No," wrote Theodore, who is enormously sensible.

I like to think how many bears would have had their heads turned by all the attention Theodore has received since his television appearances on both sides of the Atlantic. He has been deluged with offers of marriage, changes of home, and gifts. "One-Eyed Connolly" gave him a sword in case he had to go into Central Park after nightfall. "Winnie-the-Pooh" gave him a revolver for the same purpose. Other equally useful donations include a whistle (for help or taxis), a set of matching luggage, a fur brush ("girls like neat bears best"), a great deal of reading material, a pair of spectacles, scissors, and a set of eating utensils.

And Theodore himself? I find I've almost finished the book without telling you anything about Himself, who's been with me, cub and bear, for nearly twenty years now.

The one thing I know I must avoid at this point is any whimsicality or saccharine sentimentality. He'd hate that, too.

To me he is factual, and as real a part of my life as anything I possess. He doesn't remotely resemble a favorite watch or any really inanimate object and I would no more dream of going away without him, even for a night, than flying to the moon. But then I've never really fancied *that*, though I think Theodore might rather like it.

Yet I know that the same thing would happen on the moon as it does in New York, Greece, Hollywood, and East Paduka: the moment I unpack and put Theodore on my bedside table with his friends and props, the strange place becomes a kind of home. I think he's a symbol of unloneliness. He sits there on his haunches (how he *hates* standing up!) reminding me of all the happy—and unhappy—times we've had together, his funny little face lifting me when things are looking black.

Small as he is, he is a tower of strength, and both H.H. and his minute crocheted friend rely entirely on him. The three of them are sitting in front of me now with their two house guests, who are both on their first visit to Greece. Theodore, with his tiny dictionary in front of him, looks as if he's explaining the intricacies of the Greek language to them.

I suppose that if my mother *hadn't* given away my original Teddy to that rummage sale, he'd be sitting in my flat in London, alone and neglected: (a) because I wouldn't have felt the same about the species if it hadn't been for that sudden deprivation and (b) because he might have been too heavy to cart everywhere, to say nothing of the possible overweight charge involved on the plane. Though recently a twenty-five-year-old actress left London Airport for New York, clutching a Teddy Bear which was to cost her $50 in excess baggage, and an English girl who had forgotten to bring hers paid nine sterling pounds to have him shipped over later by air.

Luckily, Theodore is pretty mobile with his two-and-a-half-inch body and can easily be slipped into a pocket. He also has his own passport (another useful gift from his friend "One-Eyed Connolly"), so there's no ranagazoo at frontiers.

Although I haven't, I hope, been too sloppy about Theodore, I can fully sympathize with people who do go overboard about their friends. The most splendid thing to come out of all this rummaging into the Teddy Bear world is that hundreds of people are now less cautious about expressing emotions they might have thought would be construed as childish. In this they have been confusing the word "childish" with "childlike," which is surely one of the most endearing of qualities. Age simply doesn't enter into it! The older the friend, the more he is valued, particularly when he shows so visibly the characteristics that we all look for in friends. You have only to look at a genuine Teddy's face to see at once the loyalty, common sense, and, above all, dependability behind it.

Colonel Henderson, my favorite arctophilist, suggested some time ago that we should have a rally for the little chaps. I think that's a marvelous idea. We're considering holding one in London at the Albert Hall and one in New York. Will Madison Square Garden be too big, we ask ourselves? And what do we answer ourselves? No! The Colonel says that we shouldn't charge an entrance fee ("Everyone just bring their own Ted"). Very well, but we'd have to make our expenses by having the whole thing televised or filmed for perpetuity.

The whole prospect is pretty intoxicating. Will we be fortunate enough to see some of the all-time Greats of the Teddy Bear World there? Will Mr. Woppit and the bear who climbed the Matterhorn be able to make it? Will Elvis Presley and Dame Margot Fonteyn bring their bears, and will Buzzy, Old Ted, Sir Gangy de Brownman, and some of the other friends you've met and made in this book find their way there as well? Will Winnie-the-Pooh manage to get out of his chair in E. P. Dutton's to make the trip? And, above all, will the First Teddy, now in the Smithsonian, leave his glass case to explain the Creation to us?

In any case, I'm sure the turnout will be fantastic. You'll see animals who have survived earthquakes, shipwrecks, fires, broken homes, hospitals, and bombs, to say nothing of those who are short of fur, eyes, ears, and limbs. But in their battered faces you will be able still to recognize the indefinable magic which has made the Teddy Bear so unique and shimmering a figure throughout the last century.

Reluctantly I have to admit that not *everyone* is as dedicated to the subject as Colonel H and myself. Only the other day I received a postcard from a gentleman I had approached. It read:

> Dear Mr. Bull, I regret that I have no son with valuable information on the Teddy Bear subject. My boys have very little information on any subject. I do have a rather curious aunt in Savannah who has sent you my name. Any time you do a symposium on curious aunts, I should be glad to help.

About the Author

PETER BULL is full of surprises, full of love. The best friend of the bear, he has a family of fourteen Teddy friends in his London Chelsea flat and a family of eleven in his New York, Morningside Heights, apartment, all of whom, he complains, get into a "foul temper" when he is away from them. Mr. Bull is also known as a stage and film actor (*Dr. Strangelove*, *Dr. Dolittle*, *Tom Jones*, *Luther*) and as an author, mostly of autobiographical works.